# "You Have Lipstick on Your Teeth"

ISBN-13: 978-1490963419
ISBN-10: 1490963413

*InThePowderRoom.com*
@InThePowderRoom

Cover design by Lisa Knight, *DesignsDoneNow.com*
Editor photograph by Laura Lee Beamon

# "You Have Lipstick on Your Teeth"

### and Other Things You'll Only Hear
### from Your Friends *In The Powder Room*

## Edited by Leslie Marinelli

# Contents

This book is dedicated to all the women in our lives who love us enough to always tell the brutal truth.

# Introduction

We've all been there.

You're holding court at the dinner table with a rousing story, thinking you're captivating everyone in the group. You deliver the punchline . . . but the response is undeniably subdued. The woman opposite smiles but avoids eye contact and the hipster dude next to her shifts uneasily from one bony butt cheek to the other.

Meanwhile your best friend at the end of the table is staring wildly at you, curling her lip and licking her teeth like an anxious hyena.

WTF?

"Let's go to the ladies' room," she says with theatrical emphasis.

Once safely inside the sanctuary of the powder room, she positions you in front of the mirror and shows you the garish slash of lipstick that has managed to smear itself over your front teeth, making you look like a zombie on a bender.

As you wipe your chompers clean, you thank her and share a belly laugh about how the waiter reminds you of that guy you dated in college with the disturbing fetish for raw pizza dough.

Thank God for girlfriends and shared visits to powder rooms!

That's always been the concept behind our website *InThePowderRoom.com* where we've been entertaining women with our humor and bold, brave honesty since 2009, so it was a natural progression for us to create an anthology of original short stories from some of the wittiest women writers we know—stories they would only tell their closest friends, most likely from within the haven of a ladies' room or a Girls' Night Out.

This is a collection of 39 stories by women, for women, about being women—bodily changes, relationships, careers, motherhood, aging, illness—it's all in here, with the humor and grit that proudly sets *In The Powder Room* apart.

But be forewarned: we're holding nothing back.

We're revealing our deep dark secrets—our most embarrassing moments, our fears, our masturbating grandmas—because it is through our most vulnerable and honest moments that we forge the strongest connections with others. These connections sustain us; they're the "Me too!" moments of relief we feel when a writer bares all and we discover we aren't so alone after all.

*You have a gimpy boob?* Me too.

*You think glitter is the herpes of the craft world?* Me too!

*You had the world's worst date with the freakiest guy?* Hell to the yeah.

*You peed your pants in public?* All. The. Time.

*You got your fishnet-clad leg stuck to your head on stage in front of thousands of people?* Wait . . . what? OMG. Tell me everything!

2

So buckle up, Buttercup. We're about to let you into our "Women Only!" clubhouse where the laughter, true confessions, and wine flow freely. Yes, there will be accidents and surprises along the way, so keep an extra tampon in your purse and a posse of best friends in your speed-dial.

But do come along for the ride. We are your friends, your sisters, your mothers, and your daughters. We don't care how old you are, or what life path you've chosen. It doesn't matter to us if you have crows' feet, 36-Longs, skin tags, or diarrhea of the mouth when you get nervous. We're here to say, "Yes. Me too!" whether your vagina looks like a freshly-plucked chicken, Buckwheat in a scissor hold, or a cruciferous vegetable gone bad.

Regardless of what life has dished up for you, chances are, we've been there and we can relate. We'll help you laugh it off, or hold your hand until you're ready to laugh again.

And we promise: we'll always tell you when you have lipstick on your teeth.

*Leslie Marinelli, Editor-in-Chief*
*Diane Hayman, Co-Founder and CEO*
*In The Powder Room*

# Beauty and The Beast:
# Keeping Abreast of Sibling Rivalry

*by Leslie Marinelli*

I know it's wrong, but I can't help it.

*I have a favorite.*

I've read numerous books about siblings and birth order. All the experts agree that favoritism causes irreparable harm.

And yet, no matter how hard I try to be fair and impartial, there is one I simply like better . . .

She's prettier than her sister. There, I said it.

She's also older, so we've had more time together to bond.

Truth be told, she's simply nearer and dearer to my heart— and not just in terms of proximity.

She's my left breast, and she's spectacular.

But our family dynamic has always been a bit dysfunctional.

My breast started to develop when I was 11-years-old. And no, that's not a typo. I said *breast* . . . as in one. My left breast, "Mutt," began to bud a full year before "Jeff" on the right joined the puberty party in my Benetton sweater. And I'll never forget it, because my best friend's big sister Kelly told EVERYONE about my Lone Ranger. (Not unrelated: Kelly totally had it coming when we put that Nair in her shampoo.)

That was 1981. We were all singing about "Bette Davis Eyes," but I knew in my heart I would never be "Jessie's Girl" or experience "Endless Love" with only one hooter in my holster. A man with a "Slow Hand" sounded like a real catch according to The Pointer Sisters, but a girl with a slow breast? Not so much.

My chest ached constantly that summer . . . but mostly from the sadness over my parents' recent divorce and having to spend July and August in the face-melting heat of Phoenix, Arizona, away from my mom, dog, and friends back east.

So when I noticed a lump on the left side of my chest that July, I had no idea what to make of it. The only thing I knew about boobs was that they came in pairs. This thing must have been a spider bite, or a hula-hoop injury, or a really low-hanging goiter.

But when the soreness persisted, I decided to take matters into my own hands. Every time I went into the bathroom, I would frantically perform 2-3 sets of the "I must, I must, I must increase my bust" move . . . *but only with my right arm.* Maybe I could give my lagging right breast a jump start and it could catch up with the other one before I went back to school.

Naturally my dad and stepmom were very curious why I was spending so much time grunting in the powder room that summer.

"Honey, are you OK in there?" my stepmom asked through the door. "You sound like you're in pain. Are you eating enough fruit?"

"You know, when I was a kid, my Bubbie would line us all up on Sunday nights and make each of us swallow a spoonful of cod liver oil," my father chimed in.

"I'm fine," I'd grunt between reps. "I'll be out in a minute."

I'd emerge moments later—sweaty, breathless, right bicep bulging . . .

"Oh! Of course!" They nodded. There was only one other reason a kid that age would spend so much time behind a locked bathroom door.

After that, they gave me a wide berth . . . and told me to wash my hands a lot. Next thing I knew, my stepmom bought me a copy of *Our Bodies, Ourselves*.

I missed my mom.

My fascinating new book kept me busy though, as did exercising my right arm multiple times a day. By the end of the summer, I could properly diagnose 12 different venereal diseases and lift a car off a toddler with my left arm tied behind my back.

Surprisingly, having half an upper body like Lou Ferrigno did not nudge my other breast into existence. I returned home to Pittsburgh that August with a heavy heart and a rogue breast bud camouflaged by a "Wouldn't you like to be a Pepper too?" t-shirt.

I disguised my embarrassing deformity to the best of my 6th grade ability. Luckily for me, ruffled prairie blouses and denim vests were all the rage in the early '80s, so it really wasn't that hard to hide from most people . . . except for that bitch Kelly with the chemical burns on her scalp.

About a year later, my right breast arrived on the scene, but she was definitely the ugly stepsister to my first-born favorite—just the slightest bit smaller, and never quite as ample—with a lazy eye and a limp, if I'm being honest. To this day, sometimes I catch a glimpse of her and fully expect to hear her quoting Igor from *Young Frankenstein*: "What hump?"

By the time I got to high school, "Mutt and Jeff" had become more like "Marcia and Jan Brady." Sure, they were both flaxen-haired adolescent beauties, but we all know who got asked out on more dates.

Speaking of which, the first time I ever let a boy get to second base, it came as no surprise that he spent a lot more time hanging out with Marcia than Jan. I *told* her the lemon juice and the Afro wig were a bad idea. "Just be yourself, Jan! You'll make friends one day," I said.

Fortunately, things pretty much evened out with the girls once I went away to college and embraced an all-carb lifestyle. I still couldn't technically call them "the twins," unless they were fraternal, born over a year apart, and fathered by two different baby-daddies. But over time "Marcia and Jan" matured. Or maybe I matured. Actually, I was probably just too busy playing beer pong and dancing in fraternities to notice or care. Either way, my 1.5 breasts and I learned to live together in relative harmony.

The three of us sure had some good times together in the 1990s. We frolicked on the topless beaches of Spain, cleansed our pores in the mud baths of Mexico, skinny dipped up and down the Jersey Shore, and even discovered our aptitude for foreign currency with the breast-to-Mardi-Gras-beads exchange rate in New Orleans.

Eventually I settled down and snagged me a husband. Sure, he's legally blind without his contacts, and yes, he's right-handed, but so what? He's mine and he loves all of me unconditionally. In fact, he claims he's never noticed that one of my kumquats wears a back brace and speaks with a lisp, but whatever. He ain't no dummy. Shoot, I could have a third nipple on my face and he'd be like "Yay! Nipple. Nipple good! Three nipples—more gooder."

Clearly, marital bliss agreed with us, until I became a mother for the first time.

I'm fairly certain God designed breast-feeding as a way to distract new mothers from all the carnage down below.

When my milk came in, I stopped icing my Frankengina and marveled at the majesty of my new rack. It was truly a sight to behold. No longer were my breasts separate but unequal. They were finally one unified all-you-can-eat-buffet of womanly splendor. At last, their purpose in life would be realized and they would be judged not by their outward appearance, but by the content of their character.

What I didn't know was how difficult it would be for my newborn son and I to figure out how to properly latch-on. By the end of our first week together, my saber-toothed baby had managed to completely mangle my right nipple. "Marcia and Jan" morphed into "Beauty and The Beast." For the next two weeks, I could only nurse my son with my left udder and use a breast pump on the raw right side. "See? Even the baby has a favorite," I lamented to my mother as I applied *Lansinoh-my-God-this-fucking-HURTS!* to my uncooperative red-headed-step-nipple.

All three of my baby barracudas experienced the same passive-aggressive behavior from my right Milk Dud. And with every new bambino, "The Beast" seemed to grow more hideous and surly . . . just like Jan Brady when she had to start wearing glasses.

My breastfeeding days are long gone, but the sibling rivalry remains. Now that I'm in my 40s, my girls compete less with each other about size or popularity. Today, it's more about endurance—neither wants to get stepped on or mistaken for a genetically modified spaghetti squash. Little sister Jan has been gloating that she's finally better at something than her alpha-boob big sister Marcia, "The larger they are the harder they fall."

The important thing is that we are a family and we stick together, through all kinds of highs (that really *was* a "Miracle

Bra") and lows (topless petting zoo . . . never again). I just wish all those years of favoritism hadn't negatively impacted Jan so much. Either I'm sprouting nipple hair, or she's donning that black Afro again, bless her heart.

As different as they are, they're my girls and I'll love them until the day I die. But honest to Pete, if I hear any more "Marcia, Marcia, Marcia," I might have to put some Nair in Jan's shampoo.

*Leslie Marinelli is a writer, wife, mother of three, toilet humor aficionada, and transplanted Pittsburgher trapped in the suburbs of Atlanta. She's a weekly columnist and the Editor-in-Chief of* In The Powder Room, *as well as the creative force behind the riotous blog* The Bearded Iris: A Recalcitrant Wife and Mother Tells All. *Leslie was named a* BlogHer *Humor Voice of the Year in 2013 and 2012, and a* Babble *Top 100 Mom Blogger in 2011. Connect with Leslie and her bickering breasticles on Twitter @TheBeardedIris.*

# Jungle Moves

*by Alexandra Rosas*

How can she not know?

Every single Saturday night, it just keeps on happening and I can't *not* do anything about it anymore. She's my best friend, I have to say something. I mean, I would want her to tell me if this was about me.

Or am I fooling myself?

Who has the right to tell someone about her dancing style? I'm not Don Cornelius. You just don't appoint yourself dance floor judge and write tickets up for stripper-like dance moves.

Michelle has been my best friend since we met freshman year at our all-girl high school. I know and love everything about her, except for the everything I'm watching here tonight.

We're at Scott E's Pub, like we always are on a Saturday night. Bobby Z is deejaying and everything he throws on the turntable makes Michelle squeal, "I love this song!" I'm watching her right now, and wishing that two weeks ago, when I'd had enough liquid courage in me to sit her down and bring up how everyone stares at her on the dance floor, that I *would have actually done it.*

My plan is to do some dance floor people watching first—begin with pointing out the Soul Train Die Hards, and then work my way on to the hoochy mamas. Coyly, I'll mention someone on the dance floor doing some brazen bump-n-grind pelvic thrusts that all the horn-dogs in the place are noticing, and then I'll exclaim with surprise, "OMG! Can you believe it? That looks like some of YOUR moves. Maybe you'd better stop! See how bad it looks!"

I imagine her thanking me with a genuine wide-eyed look of gratitude, "Thank you! I had no idea! Oh my gosh, THANK YOU for saving me from looking like a strip dancer!"

Over and over, I replay this scene in my head. I convince myself it will go smooth as silk. I'm getting ready, determined to end her embarrassing ways tonight. *All right, take a deep breath now.*

The song she's thrusting to is hitting its last beats. Oh Lord help me, she is waiting until the last drop of it—boom—working the imaginary pole between her legs like she's getting paid by the second. The writhing and neck rolling that the entire pub and I are being treated to right now leaves me with no question. It goes down tonight. No more hoochy mama, no more free tips on how to be a pro stripper on the floor from my best friend. I am the only one who can save her from what people are thinking about her, and I am going to do just that.

The thrust stops here.

I'll just wait out a few more sexy bass beats of "I Heard It Through the Grapevine"—*my God but that's a hot song—I wish I had the balls to be out there dancing right now.* Anyway, she'll be back at our table any second now, and thank God because it is killing me to hear the guys behind me while they watch her, "Dude! Awesome! Amateur stripper night!"

Dum dum dumdumdum . . . Dum. *Honey, honey yeah.* And the moment of truth is just about to get real. The song is over and I see her smiling and tossing her hair, she's heading back to me.

Here we go.

"Whoo. Man. It's hot in here. You wanna beer? I'll get us some . . ."

"Um. No. Yeah, Michelle . . . let's just sit. I wanna talk to you."

"Well, we can sit and drink, so . . ."

"No. It's good, let's sit."

"Suit yourself. But I'm thirsty. HOT BEAT. Man, that's a hot beat. God, I love dancing."

*Aaargh.* How can I say anything now? She LOVES dancing. But I have to. I just can't let her move like she's used to going home with a hundred singles stuffed into her panties.

"So, Michelle, I want to talk to you about something. It's kind of hard to bring up."

"Oh my gosh. What? Are you OK? You're not pregnant, are you? Please don't tell me it's that loser Michael's. He's so boring. I'll do anything you need!"

"No no no. NO. This is about . . . you. And some stuff. And what's wrong with Michael? We've been together for almost four years."

"Eck. He's gross. Is it about that guy two weeks ago? Oh, can't we forget about that? It's not like I do it all the time."

*Dang.* I think to myself. Another subject to broach.

"No, no, umm . . . I'm just going to come out and say it. It's about the way you dance."

"My dancing? What are you talking about? You are so weird. MY DANCING?"

"Yeah. Michelle, you dance like a GD stripper."

"Ha! OMG. You are so funny. I love it when you drink. You think I'm that good? *Awesome*."

I open my mouth to plead my case, and then I realize, I'm dead because Morris Day comes on. No way she's going to listen to me now.

"Jungle Love! My favorite song!" Michelle screams and grabs my hand. She pulls me out into the middle of the small bar's dance floor and with her hands on her hips, she begins to rock it. Every guy in the bar looks up. And I fear guilty stripper status by association. I feel everyone's eyes on us.

And then I look at her—how can she not notice that everyone's looking at us? But when I look at her, I see that she sees . . . no one. She is lost in the music and in the moment and she doesn't notice any of the things *I* notice. Or maybe she does. And she just doesn't give a shit.

Ah, my wonderful hip shaking friend, Michelle. I guess hips don't lie.

I need to talk to you about something all right, Michelle. I need to ask you to teach me how to not give a shit. I think about all the fun I miss out on because I worry about what people will say, what they'll think. That they'll talk about me. And just as I finally figure out it's me who needs the talking to, Morris Day sends me a subliminal kiss: *Come on, baby, where's your guts?*

Yup, another Saturday night, and me and my girl Michelle "Hips Don't Lie" Shakira are on the dance floor at Scott E's Pub. We're working it hard and everybody's watching. Just call me "Don't Give a Shit" Sugar tonight.

We'll dance it up until the last song drops. And then we'll head out for breakfast, a big one too, because the way we're owning the floor, we're leaving here with a shit-ton of singles.

*Alexandra is a first-generation American who has been writing memoir and humor since 2006.* BlogHer *named her a 2011 Voice of the Year for Humor, a 2012 Voice of The Year for Parenting, and a 2013 Voice of the Year for Heart. Alexandra has been published in various humor and writing websites and is a regular contributor for* Aiming Low, Sprocket Ink, Funny not Slutty, TikiTiki Blog, *and* MilwaukeeMoms. *A* Babble *Top 100 Mom Blogger, you can find her living online at her personal blog* Good Day, Regular People, *and offline with her husband and three children in Cedarburg, Wisconsin. Connect with her on Twitter @GDRPempress.*

# Round-Headed Baby

*by Mere Smith*

For the record, I didn't plan on doing it in a TGI Friday's bathroom.

The *plan* was to get her drunk on frozen margaritas, then do it at her house.

My timing's always been rotten.

*brushbrushbrushbrushbrush*

The sound was comforting, something I'd heard all my life.

We were out to dinner alone for once. Her giant purse slumped near the sink, mouth gaping like a fake leather whale. The smell of her Chanel No. 5 hovering, pleasant, in the air.

Reckon I was just lulled, is all, 'cause suddenly I found myself dragging a deep breath up, up outta my bowels, which were already starting to cramp.

My intestines hate confrontation.

"So, Momma?"

"Yes, sugar?"

*brushbrushbrushbrushbrush*

Leaning against the bathroom wall, I watched her in the mirror, thinking, *There ain't a damn tangle left in there, woman. I doubt your hair's had a tangle since JFK went to Dallas, when outta shock maybe you forgot to brush it for a half-hour.*

"I gotta tell you somethin'."

"You know you can tell me anything, lovie."

*brushbrushbrushbrushbrush*

"Yeah, but I don't think you'll be happy 'bout it."

"Don't be ridiculous. No matter what, I'll always be your momma, and you'll always be my perfect little round-headed baby."

She flipped her blonde hair to the other shoulder—

*brushbrush*

—and my colon started writhing.

I've always loved being Mom's round-headed baby.

The oldest of four, I'm a C-section kid of the '70s—back when they didn't give women like my mom (who stands a whopping 4'11") a choice. The doctor simply informed her, "You're too tiny to give birth. Your hips are too narrow. And aren't you lucky we live in an age where I can make that decision for you and gut you like a hog? Totally for *your* benefit, of course."

And since women weren't permitted to question their male doctors, my mom answered, "Well, I'm sure you know what's best," and took another drag off her Kool Filter King.

She and the doctor probably shared the same ashtray.

As a result, when my head didn't get smooshed by any sort of actual "birthing" process, when the doctor showed her my screaming-alien face while she was still splayed out on the surgical table—red steaming insides wide open to the air, stoned off her face on barbiturates—like a blue-masked God he rumbled, "Jaime? JAIME! Ah, there you are. Here's your perfect little round-headed baby."

And that's all Mom can remember of my birth.

So she hangs onto it.

I'm almost 40 now, and I hang onto it, too.


No, it was the "baby" part that got me.

Again my intestines spasmed, sharp.

Ironic, but I bet it felt like labor.


*brushbrushbrushbrushbrush*

My mother's hair is only a few inches past her shoulders, yet her idea of "brushing it" is more like "violently cheese-grating it until the hair apologizes."

Truly, I do not know how she has any follicles left in her scalp. Especially since I've never once glimpsed her natural hair color. For the longest time I thought "Lori Awl" was one of her friends—a friend she talked to on the phone every month behind her closed bedroom door. When I finally caught on, I asked why she didn't just chuck it, let her hair grow out instead of submitting it to constant bleach-burning root maintenance. After all, who cared about a few grays?

My mother said she'd rather be dead than old.


"I've decided I'm not having kids."

*brushb—*

She froze mid-stroke, eyes flicking up to mine in the mirror, wearing the confused look of someone who's misheard something impossible. As if the sound of her hair-brushing had drowned out my real sentence, which was obviously along the lines of, "Momma, I am pregnant with forty-eleven kids."

Though *that*, she'da been jim-dandy fine with.

But as the only person who's known me my entire life—literally, since half of me was tucked away in her ovary while she was in her *own* mother's womb—she could tell from my face that she hadn't misheard. She turned around slow, staring, brush hand drooping, before—

*"Mere! What* on *earth* are you *talkin'* 'bout?"

*The pitch-climb*, I groaned inward. *Shoulda heard it coming.*

Unique to Southern women, the pitch-climb is a constant shinnying-up of the voice that keeps all its sweetness, but inevitably translates to, *Why bless your heart, poor thing, you're just plain dumb as two rocks tryin' to fuck, huh?*

"The thing is," I floundered, "I like my life."

"But you don't know what you're *missin'* yet."

"And I don't wanna give it up."

"But it's so *worth* it."

"I'm almost 40—"

*"Plenty* a time nowdays."

"'Sides I'd probably just mess 'em up."

*"Everybody* worries about—"

*Fine. Both barrels, then?*

"Mom, I don't *want* them."


Her whole face scrunched inward as she gazed at me, suspicious.

"Is Paul makin' you do this?"

I laughed, too loud, the echo rocketing off empty paper towel dispensers and the abyss of Mom's bottomless purse. And OK, so it might've been a little hysterical. Plus at this point I felt like I was gonna muck my drawers.

"He's not 'makin'' me do anything," I assured her. "Paul and I've talked about it a hundred times. If anything, I think *he* still wants 'em."

"Then—"

"Then nothin'," I snapped. "*I don't.*"

She flinched.

That's when I glanced over her shoulder and saw my face in the mirror...

I looked mean as hell.

Hell, I *was* mean as hell, making my own mother flinch. Had to be good news for all those unborn baby souls picking out parents, that someone like me wouldn't be in the lineup.

I tried joking, "And you can't make me."

There was a pause, before my mom stepped close and put her brush-hand on my arm, bristles scratching my shirt. For some reason that prickly sensation made me wanna burst into tears.

"Oh, *honey.*"

And there it was, in one word. An endearment, no less.

Guess I shoulda expected that, too.

See, along with the pitch-climb, those of us born under the Mason-Dixon know that most words last longer than those miserly Yanks will allow. The word "hi," for example, can contain up to four syllables, depending on dialect. In fact, our language is a lot like Chinese—with vocal tones that convey subtext only to others who speak fluent Southern.

So when my mother said, "Oh, *honey*"—and didn't skimp on any of its seven syllables—I knew what that really meant:

That's plumb crazy!

You'd make a great mother!

How could you do this to me?

Did you wait too long?

But I only have four grandchildren from your brothers and
sister!

What woman doesn't have kids if she can?

Are you sayin' I wasn't a good mother?

Are you hidin' something?

I want you to have everything!

Why're you so goddamn ornery?

You will regret this forever!

But your children would be so beautiful!

What about your familial duty?

Everyone fucks 'em up, though!

Why didn't you tell me sooner?

But are you *really* sure?

Are you chicken?

Don't be selfish!

Well if that's what you want . . .

But if my oldest is too old to have kids, what does that make
*me*?

I love you.

No matter what.

Without warning, someone tightened the muffler clamp from
a '77 Ford pickup 'round my windpipe.

My dad drove a '77—he called it The Beast—so I knew what
that muffler clamp looked like, and now, how it felt constricting my

throat—not to mention the space in my head where the water is stored, because that got squoze out my eyes.

"Momma—" I strangled.

We both waited. I couldn't finish.

And if she didn't move that hellfired brush off my arm, I was going to lose my shit right here in a TGI Friday's bathroom.

Maybe both ways.

"Why don't you go get us some margaritas, lovie?"

Now *I* was confused.

"Some—what—did you hear what I said?" I asked.

"Sure, honey, I heard ya. I'm not deaf." She wiped my cheeks with her free hand, patted 'em. "G'on now. Go find us a booth and some margaritas."

"Don't you wanna—I don't know. *Talk* about this?"

My mom smiled wide, trying so hard to hide her heart.

But I've known her my whole life.

"Momma—"

"G'on, then. And don't forget the—"

"Salt," I finished. "I know."

"'Round the rims. And *frozen* margaritas. They're like Slurpees for winos."

"I know."

"Then buzz off, little bee. Whatcha waitin' for, engraved invitation?"

Not knowing what else to do, I grabbed the bathroom door, pulled.

The blastwave of chain-restaurant noise stunned me like a cattle bolt.

I turned back. "You OK, Momma?"

"Sure, baby," she said to the mirror. "I'm just gonna brush my hair real quick."

*Mere Smith is a recovering Southerner, as well as a longtime TV writer (*Angel, Rome*), author (*Cowface, The Blood Room*), and blogger. She can be found at EvilGalProductions.com, or on Twitter @EvilGalProds.*

# Swinging Singles

*by Abby Heugel*

My grandma was married when she was 18, and the fact that I'm in my early 30s and still single baffles her mind, as do people who refrigerate their perishable items.

*"If it's cooked, it can never go bad."*

But fearing I have a metaphorical "Best If Used By" date stamped on my forehead, she feels compelled to offer these gems:

*"Don't be so stubborn. He doesn't have to look like a movie star, but you don't want ugly kids."*

*"You have to spice things up. I remember your grandpa would come downstairs while I was doing the washing and bend me over the washing machine. Sometimes I was annoyed, but it never lasted long enough for me to care."*

*"If you're in a car with a man and he starts to get fresh with his hands, tell him to knock it off. If he doesn't listen, open the door and kick his ass out of the car. Tell him to go find a floozy on the avenue and then take yourself out for ice cream."*

Well-played, old woman. Well-played.

But she isn't alone in her well-meaning yet antiquated advice. Friends who used to encourage me to do the splits on the railing of a bar deck or ask me to help them get thongs out of a tree are now married and offering to set me up with a cousin who has "most of his hair" and a weekend pass.

While I appreciate the concern about my possible life as a spinster, I'm not worried at all. In fact, I prefer being single and boring.

I know, I know.

Instead of painting my bathroom I could be out painting the town red in search of a husband or choreographing sex swing routines. But the thing is that . . .

a.) I fall walking up the stairs, so a sex swing would guarantee some type of self-mutilation,

b.) my commitment level extends to that of a plant in my house—and it's fake, and

c.) sex doesn't really matter to me.

*(Gasp!)*

OK. Perhaps I should rephrase that. Sex *with other people* doesn't matter much to me. Is that better?

I remember getting "The Talk" when I was younger and being equally horrified and amused by what I was told. I don't think I believed it. As someone who thought you could get pregnant by kissing, the truth sounded ridiculous to me.

But my suspicions were confirmed when I came upon the book, *"Where Did I Come From?"* at a friend's house. For those unfamiliar with this text, it's "The Talk" illustrated with very anatomically correct cartoon characters.

My friend and I flipped through it *(over and over)* with a mix of curiosity and skeptical laughter, amazed that people did that stuff on purpose. One image that's burned into my brain is that of the two naked cartoon adults standing next to a bathtub in all their bare-assed glory.

The decorative throw rug in that minuscule bathroom did nothing to distract from the tufts of hair strategically highlighted in lower extremities or the sagging body parts so openly displayed. These exhibitionists were smiling because they knew they were about to change the lives of children everywhere. With a turn of the page, there was no going back, no "unknowing" the things they were about to illustrate so happily through careful word choice and stark illustrations.

But while the book gave us the basics, I realize now as a *(semi-experienced)* adult that it left a few details out.

Unless it's gigantic, a bathtub is rarely romantic or large enough to accommodate two adults of average size with any degree of comfort. If by some miracle he squeezes in, there will be no water left in the tub. She will be cold, and additionally, she will be pissed because the floor will be flooded.

He will counter with the fact that less water means more room for lovin' and continue his advances, at which time she will remind him that if there was less of him to "love" and he actually ate the healthy lunches she sent to work with him each day, they might not have this problem.

Knowing he's in a rather vulnerable position, he will gingerly counter with the fact that *she* is actually taking up the majority of the room in the tub—but that he still wants to fluff those fleshy pillows, if she's in the mood.

She will not be in the mood.

In fact, she will be drying herself off with a towel, muttering about how her mother was probably right and double-checking to make sure she has adequate AA batteries in the nightstand.

A man on a mission, he will set off to find a mop to rectify the situation. Realizing he doesn't know where they keep the mop—and wisely keeping this information to himself—he will resort to towels.

An hour later, with his attempts to clean the floor complete, he will then proceed to enter the living room to show off how he has created a human towel rack with a certain member of his anatomy.

She'll be on the couch watching back episodes of *The Bachelor* and feeding her feelings with Fritos.

OK.

That's probably a generalization I've gleaned through personal experience, my married friends, and poor sitcom choices. But that's no more misguided than thinking I need to get married to be somehow complete. I have adequate AA batteries in the nightstand, thank you very much.

If anything, I have decided I want to be a Trophy Wife. Well, perhaps I should rephrase that. I have decided I want to be a Consolation Prize Wife, which is like a Trophy Wife, but actually way cooler because she requires less maintenance.

The typical Trophy Wife is young and married to an older powerful man—the Sugar Daddy—and serves as a visual status symbol of his success. She's basically arm candy. I'm not quite as young or as hot, but I'm thinking I might be able to swing the alternative here.

As a Consolation Prize Wife, I could still marry a powerful man and serve as a visual *(or vocal, more likely)* status symbol of his humble success. He would make enough money so that I could be a stay-at-home-mom minus the kids, work on my exotic container gardens and tirelessly devote myself to perfecting the slow motion *Baywatch* jog.

I would be required to get dressed up and attend various social events with him—*I make a great party date*—and in return, he would be required to be handy around the house, request no emotional attachment or sexual interest unless provoked (by me) and have a Canadian accent.

The last point is somewhat negotiable.

It's a total win-win. My grass would get cut, and he would always have a witty party date.

Plus, my concerned friends and family could rest easy knowing I'm not resigned to the life of a spinster, but rather that of a companion to a man with one foot in the grave and another on a banana peel, who knows that I prefer bathing alone and long walks to the fridge.

And as a Consolation Prize Wife, I would make it my duty to remain faithful until death do us part, at which time I will be back to where I started from.

Which will be, most likely, the couch—or doing the splits on the deck railing of a bar.

Hey, I'm still young and single.

*Abby Heugel is an editor for employment, and an award-winning humor writer and blogger at AbbyHasIssues.com for enjoyment. Her work has been featured on* The Huffington Post, Erma Bombeck Writers' Workshop, *and other websites, but she doesn't want to brag. However, she considers the fact that she has managed to keep her fake tree alive for almost five years, and can still do the splits all three ways, among her greatest accomplishments. Connect with her on Twitter @AbbyHasIssues.*

# There Is No Ball Drying at the Dinner Table

*by Noa Gavin*

When I moved in with my husband, there was nothing to prepare me for the grossness of manhood. Perhaps if I'd grown up with brothers or a shameless dad, I would have been prepared to be married to a man. Instead, I grew up with a quiet mother and a sister who valued privacy and the most basic idea of decorum.

I don't consider myself a prudish person, and have gained a reputation as someone without shame. I will do anything, say anything, take a joke way over the line without a second thought. I've gotten in a fistfight with a very tall and very fabulous drag queen at a bachelorette party. I was asked to leave a bar for telling the waitress that she'd front-wedged her vulva and her skirt was short enough for the entire bar to see. I've gotten my family forcibly ejected from a Christopher & Banks (for life!) for referring to nuns and anal sex in the same sentence.

I am a tornado of public indecency.

As a result of a lifetime of impropriety, I thought there was literally nothing my husband could do to gross me out. I'd seen and done it all. My strong appetite for terribleness combined with the love and butterflies and bullshit of being a newlywed would ne'er let a disgusting habit interfere in our house of love!

Then one day, while I sat in the living room quietly reading, my husband propped his leg up on the couch, and gently toweled off his balls after a shower while discussing the credit card bill.

How wrong I was. How could this man just stand there going over the budget like he wasn't delicately dabbing his scrotum with a very nice towel fresh off our registry?

The first few months of marriage were a cold dickslap to the face about just how well we'd really "get to know one another." At first, I said nothing about his repulsive habits. I didn't want to be "that wife," who disallowed her husband's basic human actions because it bothered her. That's what *Cosmo*-reading *Bravo*-heads did! I was a cool wife. I wasn't a nagging wife. I could deal with this. Right?

Then he took a shit while I was in the shower right next to him, and I was done. Nope. I couldn't do this anymore. He was so gross it was hurting my soul, and I realized that if I was going to make it in this marriage, some boundaries about grossness would have to be set.

I threw back the shower curtain and let my rage fly.

"YOU HAVE TO STOP BEING SO GROSS. I CAN'T TAKE IT ANYMORE!"

He looked up at me, a little dazed at being shouted at mid-poop, and put his phone down.

"What are you talking about?" he asked.

"You are gross. I love you, but you are so gross it hurts. You are pooping while I am showering. I can smell it, and I want to die."

"I . . . um, well, I can't just stop now."

Frustrated at the reality of the situation, I started to cry like a wuss, overwhelmed with ridiculous disappointment.

"It's not just this," I whimpered. "It's your ball-drying and your dick-scratching and you leaving the door open when you poop and pooping while I'm in the bathroom at all and farting without a second thought and sitting naked on the white couch and your spitting in the sink and it is so awful."

"You can be gross too," he said quietly, defensive of what I'm sure were lifelong habits that plenty of girlfriends had put up with. Not me. Not now.

"Oh? When was the last time you saw anything of my vagina other than sex? When was the last time you had to bear witness to tampon insertion and/or removal? When was the last time I used your special towel to dry my puss while I paid bills? When was the last time you even knew I pooped at all?" I shouted, still standing in the running shower and throwing water everywhere for emphasis.

His face twisted in disgust at my words, which only added fuel to my rage-fire. *Oh those things are gross, huh? You bastard.*

"Look, babe, I don't know what you want from me," he said, still sitting on the toilet. "I have to dry my balls, I have to spit, I have to fart, I have to poop, and sometimes my dick itches. It's going to happen. Deal with it."

I stomped my foot and nearly slipped. "No. No, not OK. I'm not asking for much, I'm asking for you never to do those things in front of me. For the love of all that is holy and for the sanctity of our marriage, please don't do this to me."

"I don't scratch my dick to piss you off!"

"It feels like a personal affront to my eyes and my sensibilities."

He raised his eyebrows and crossed his arms over his chest indignantly.

"Yeah? Well sometimes your boobs itch, and you scratch them in front of me," he snapped.

"The difference is, you like that, and I am repulsed by dick scratching."

He sighed heavily, slid the shower curtain closed in front of me, and flushed. I heard him leave the bathroom, and sure that I had pissed him off, I cried even harder. I could do almost everything else involved with marriage, I was up for the challenge, but I could not handle this. I believe that there are certain lines you should never cross with anyone. Ball-drying at eye-level is a huge, bold-faced red line of awful.

The bathroom door opened, and he came back in with a notepad and a pen in his hand.

"Fine. I'll give you this one—but we're *both* going to set some rules here. You don't want to see this from me, and there are things I never, ever want to see from you."

So, with me in the shower and him leaning against the sink, we set rules about grossness that have kept the peace—and a level of mystery that is both welcome and necessary—for years.

### The Rules

*His:*

> No ball drying and/or dick scratching outside the bathroom
> No pooping with the door open or with a witness
> No spitting in the sink without a minimum five seconds of water running

No attempting to fart like a monster all the goddamned
time

*Hers:*
No "vaginal grossness" with him as a witness under any
circumstances (barring childbirth)
No attempting to fart like a monster in bed
No saying the word "queef," ever

I learned quickly in my marriage that there is such a thing as
"too close," and we will never have to experience that. Now I love
that disgusting bastard all the more.

*Noa Gavin is a writer/improv comedian from Dallas, TX. Noa
always wanted to be a comedian, having been raised on Carol
Burnett, Lucille Ball, and* Saturday Night Live *and being generally
unfit for "normal" work. She got her start being professionally
funny on her comedy blog,* OhNoa.com *and was chosen as a
BlogHer* Humor Voice of The Year in 2011. *Noa trained in improv
at* Dallas Comedy House, *where she regularly performs sketch
and improv. Connect with her on Twitter @OhNoaG.*

# The (Not So) High Price of Fashion

*by Wendi Aarons*

Not too long ago, I attended a very nice cocktail party with some very nice people and while there, I met a sophisticated older woman named Margaret. We chatted about this and that, and I found myself quietly marveling at how impeccable she was in her appearance. Gorgeous hair, flawless make-up and understated, yet just-stylish-enough jewelry. There wasn't a single inch of her that wasn't polished and shined to perfection. Next to her, I had all the panache of a female dockworker after a nine-day steroid binge.

But after we'd been talking awhile, I felt comfortable enough to lean in close, grab the sleeve of her silk turquoise dress and lightly rub it between my thumb and middle finger while gushing about how beautiful it was. At that moment, Margaret could have easily signaled a cater-waiter to come escort me into the kitchen and dunk me in the deep fat fryer, but instead, she immediately flashed a huge, conspiratorial grin at me. And then she ran her hands down her slim hips and loudly crowed, "Twenty bucks! TJ Maxx! Can you believe it?"

Because that's what we women do: we tell each other exactly how much our clothes cost. But only, and this is important, if they didn't cost too much.

"Oh, this sweater? Target clearance rack. Ten bucks."

"My shoes? Found 'em at a flea market and paid the guy fifty cents and a piece of used chewing gum."

"No, darling, my earrings aren't actually from Rodeo Drive. They're from the ears of the dead hooker I found behind a mulberry bush at the reservoir. It's *such* a shame her pimp took the matching bracelet."

What's the point of being a brilliant bargain hunting cheapass if you can't share it with everyone?

Of course, before you can brag about your great deals, you have to *find* your great deals. And I learned how to do just that from my mom, Sharon. My mom is my personal shopping hero and not just because she once had so many coupons and discount codes in her hand when buying a pair of shoes at Kohl's, they actually had to pay *her* $2 to take them home. (And don't think I haven't heard that particular story about a million times.)

But it was my mom who taught my sisters and me at a very young age to immediately head to the back of the store where the sale racks are located. "Don't bother making eye contact with the clerks," she said, "because those teenage morons are just going to slow you down with their dumb greetings and stupid sweater folding. You're there on serious business. Don't forget it."

And she was totally right because it was there, in the badly-lit back areas of stores, that I found shorts for 50% off, tank tops for 60% off and swimsuits on Final Clearance. Sure, it might have been January at the time, but I knew I could shove my purchases into the back of my closet for a few months, then show off my savvy shopping skills as soon as the snow melted. And if anything gives you a boost of confidence in a bikini, it's strutting around the pool knowing you paid just $5 for it when everyone else paid $75 for theirs. Suckers.

Unfortunately, however, this strategy sometimes backfires. Like the time I ordered a bunch of Team USA 2004 Olympic wear online because it was marked down 70%. It wasn't until weeks later when we opened the box stamped repeatedly with the words "No Returns," that I realized I'd actually bought Team Canada 2004 Olympic wear. As in giant, red maple leaves. As in the country we don't actually live in. As in probably the last thing most residents of Austin, Texas would trot around town proudly wearing on their chests. So for the past nine years, my husband and I have had to continually say things like, "No, I'm not actually from Canada. No, I don't even know where Ottawa is. No, I'm not related to Celine Dion and I have no idea how good the speed skating team is this year. No, I—OH, FOR THE LOVE OF GOD, WOULD YOU JUST LEAVE ME AND MY THREE DOLLAR CANADIAN MOUNTIE HOODIE ALONE?"

But while it's perfectly acceptable for women to immediately tell a stranger how little we paid for our skirt ("Sixteen bucks at Ross Dress for Less! And it's not even damaged or covered in mouse semen!"), it's never OK to tell someone you paid a lot for your clothes. Like that awful woman who was on *The Real Housewives of Beverly Hills* a few seasons ago. I seem to remember her name was Labradoodle, but that might be wrong. Anyway, during one memorable party scene, she pointed to her jeweled sunglasses and proudly said, "Like 'em? Twenty five thousand dollars!" Oh, yes, Labradoodle did.

Of course the show's viewers were disgusted by that announcement, but so were the other Beverly Hills Housewives. And not because they're frugal, sensible women, either, because they most definitely are not. No, they were disgusted because it's one thing to pay that much for an accessory and it's another thing entirely to brag about it. Had Ladradoodle said she was wearing Gymboree aviator sunglasses pilfered from her toddler's Lil' Aviator outfit like, *ahem*, someone I know once did, they would have totally applauded her thriftiness. (And then they would have taken the drink out of her hand, told her she looked like a demented bush pilot and driven her to the closest Sunglass Hut for Ray-Bans.) (I'm guessing.)

I've often asked myself why women feel compelled to tell each other how little we paid for our clothes whenever we're complimented on them. Is it because we want to appear modest? Is it because we feel awkward accepting kind words? Is it the thrill of the bargain? Or is it simply because, in the spirit of sisterhood, we want to give others the chance to run to the nearest Marshalls and snap up their own $15 pair of Kenneth Cole leather boots that are almost but not really still in style? I'm not sure.

What I do know is that the next time someone tells me how much they like my shirt, I'm going to try my best to just smile and nod and say, "Thank you." And keep it to myself that I only paid $3 for it after finding it in the very back of the store, underneath the ass of a passed out security guard named Jerry.

*Wendi Aarons is an award-winning humor writer and blogger who lives in Austin, Texas with her husband and two sons. She has written for a number of publications including* McSweeney's *and* Esther's Follies, *Austin's famous comedy revue. She is the 2012 winner of "Funniest Blog" from* Parents Magazine, *a writer for the* US Weekly *Fashion Police and has spoken on humor writing at the* BlogHer, Mom Com *and* Mom 2.0 *conferences.*

*Wendi is also the co-producer/director of the live stage show* Listen To Your Mother Austin, *and is one of the creators of* The Mouthy Housewives (MouthyHousewives.com) *and the much-lauded Twitter feed @PaulRyanGosling.*

# Drunken Botox

*by Poppy Marler*

It was never my intention to be sitting on the table of a medi-spa in a strip mall while a woman in a white coat with questionable credentials wielded a syringe toward my crow's foot. When I woke up that morning and checked my smart phone I was greeted with birthday wishes from a hundred of my closest Facebook friends, not an iCal reminder of a pending appointment to get toxins injected into my face.

My plan for the day included a boozy birthday lunch with my best girlfriend before an early movie. Unfortunately the movie plan was aborted in favor of a third champagne martini, which seemed like an excellent idea at the time.

Stumbling out the door and into the bright daylight of our small town felt like hitting the early morning after a rave. I tried to claim my unsteady gait was the result of being roofied until my friend lovingly pointed out that no one actually talked to us and we were standing in the parking lot alone.

With no movie to see and in no shape to drive home, our options were limited to shopping in the high-end strip mall in our low rent town. It didn't take long to tire of the fancy textiles, dishes, and dirty looks from nervous shopkeepers as we fondled their delicates. Undoubtedly we had doubled their door dings by walking into their little shops, but we had been pegged correctly as not-so-serious customers.

We had almost made it to the end of the shopping row when a sign on a sandwich board captured my attention. I had seen it before and had given it the side-eye several times in passing. I never stopped to actually look for fear others might notice my extreme interest. But just because I had never seriously considered squandering the grocery money on a few facial fillers while sober, didn't mean I wasn't intrigued.

After standing outside of the premises for a few minutes and then pressing my forehead to the glass, I convinced my friend we should investigate. I had read enough inserts in fashion magazines to know I was seeking information about Juvederm or Restylane. My problem areas, or so I thought, were the lines around my mouth. I had resisted many a Groupon for Botox because only one crow had landed and my forehead wrinkles didn't bother me. When I focused on my flaws in the mirror, my eyes were always drawn toward my mouth.

Knowing this information, I'm still not sure why I fully cooperated and consented to repeated demands of making "angry eyes" while being injected with 19 cc of Botox in the forehead. In fact, I giggled throughout the entire process, so apparently I never considered it could actually be motor oil.

In fact, I think it is entirely possible that the employees from the medi-spa may have supplied the Rufilin to the waiters at the restaurant. If I had looked closely I probably would have noticed their pupils actually had dollar signs. If I were paying attention I would have heard the doors automatically lock behind me and wonder why the retractable bars on the windows raised the moment we entered. I reeked of birthday desperation and was just wrinkled enough. They weren't letting me go.

Obviously my decision-making process throughout the experience is a little hazy. I read all the literature thoroughly—right after I got home—and a BUI (Botox Under the Influence) is definitely not a recommended procedure. I am completely responsible for my own stupid actions, but shame on the medi-spa for performing the procedure on a woman whose extreme inebriation was more apparent than the furrows on her brow.

To this day I am still unclear about how I went from marionette line facial fillers to Botulism between the eyes, so definitely shame on me too. I remember that after my debit card had been swiped they called someone into the office to perform the procedure. I'm hoping it was at least a nurse, but I truly have no idea. Perhaps the receptionist just put on a white jacket. Sadly, I wouldn't have known the difference.

Talk about buyer's remorse. Leaving the medi-spa with my pamphlet of fucked up side effects, Dixie Cup of water, and needled forehead was equivalent to any walk of shame. I might as well have had my bra in my pocket. Sure, I had talked about getting Botox before. In much the same way I talked about getting a tramp stamp: *conceptually.*

As someone who gives herself Bell's palsy applying false lashes, I was positive all side effects would happen to me. Just like a '50s housewife, the only thing I was more afraid of than imminent full facial paralysis was my husband's reaction. My husband has a knack for pointing out pinched newscasters and pulled actors so I was sure he would disapprove of my new look.

Though I fully planned on invoking the tenets of marital math, I knew he also wouldn't be pleased with how much I had spent. Instead, I declared the "Don't Ask, Don't Tell" policy as it was a definite state of emergency, and hoped he wouldn't notice.

Even though the brochure said it could take up to two weeks to kick in, I found myself in front of the mirror every ten minutes attempting to recreate "angry eyes." As the evening progressed it became increasingly difficult. Though I didn't notice a big difference visually, tactilely the sensation was unusual. My husband made no comment on my appearance.

The next morning when I made my way to the mirror I was relieved to see both of my eyes were open and tracking, but alarmed I couldn't move the muscles in my forehead. Most of us have done something we're not proud of while imbibing. Perhaps we divulged a juicy secret, got a little too loud, or even threw up on a bridesmaid. Those actions are cringe-worthy for a day or two. Drunken Botox lasts four months.

For the next two weeks I did what any reasonable person who just dropped a fat roll on Botox would do: I wore a hat so no one would notice. Eventually I stopped wearing the hat and still no one noticed. Not even my husband who I presume enjoyed his four-month respite from any sort of "angry eyes."

I was thankful I escaped my BUI without any serious side effects. Luckily the consequences were only a little paranoia and a hit to my pocketbook. This little incident made me wonder, though, if I was still doing this shit at 38, how I ever survived my 20s.

*Poppy is a runner, writer, and mother of three. In between Nyquil martini benders and triathlon training, she can be counted on to look up from her iPhone long enough to shuttle a teenager to the mall or dole out requisite maternal affection. Poppy blogs at the hilariously underrated parenting blog,* FunnyOrSnot.com, *and healthy lifestyle blog,* Facing40.com. *Connect with her on Twitter @PoppyJMarler.*

# The ABC Club

*by Amy Flory*

I never would have suspected on my first day of college that I would become a member of what has been famously dubbed "quite the threesome." In a maid of honor speech at our friend Bridgett's wedding, my gorgeous, but not so eloquent friend Kate bestowed this title on the three of us. After the jeers and catcalls quieted, she explained that we were unlikely, yet deeply bonded, friends. I don't believe in love at first sight, so I'm not surprised our relationship took some time to grow. We were friends before we were soul mates, and our bond is stronger for it. I really should send flowers to our college housing authority for putting us together, and kicking off a nearly 20-year love story that is still going strong.

It began back in 1995. Kate and I were high school friends turned college roommates. Bridgett lived down the hall and became a friend after impressing us with her glorious singing voice and her horrifyingly crude AOL chat room behavior. The online personas she could conjure on a whim were truly a gift. Her scathing commentary on some of our neighbors was magnificent, and in her I felt I had found a true shit-talking partner. Her theatrical background fascinated me, and her penchant for frequently breaking into song and dance made me blush.

Kate was the kind one. She was beautiful inside and out, and it was completely obvious why people regularly fell in love with her. She was kind to strangers, welcoming to outsiders, and earnest in her belief in the good of others. She was a skilled gymnast, and she carried herself with the grace of a dancer. She usually laughed at my meanness, but it always made her feel uncomfortable. Luckily, she loved me anyway.

We hated each other's boyfriends and strongly disliked each other's music choices (Enya for Kate, Barry Manilow for Bridgett, and country for me), but we bonded over a shared love of broken Doritos, cookie dough, pizza (yes we got fat, why do you ask?), and Danish cigarettes that we smoked while dangling halfway out of our dorm windows. Despite our differences, we melded perfectly.

One night, over a shared 22-ounce bottle of Pyramid Apricot Ale that we'd begged an upperclassman to buy for us, we discussed another thing we agreed on: BJs are gross. We were happy to lick Dorito dust off our fingers, but licking another person's privates? No, thank you.

That night, we formed a club: The Anti-Blowjob Club. Bridgett got to be the president, as she had never actually performed the act, with Kate and I receiving worthless titles only dirty little former-knob-slobbers deserved. Secretary and Treasurer, maybe? Sergeant-at-Arms and Social Chair? It didn't matter. We only had that one meeting, and our singular agenda was to keep our faces above the belt. We talked about having shirts made, but we had spent the last of our walking around money on the beer. After a couple of weeks, we forgot about the club, but we all held our commitment to the mission statement: *Smoking the Johnson is nasty. Don't do it.*

Our college had a strong and proud Mom's Weekend and Dad's Weekend tradition. Not Parents' Weekend. That's for pansies. We separate the grown-ups, because every kid knows it's easier to talk one parent rather than two into something questionable.

Mom's Weekend was (and still is) one of the wildest weekends of the year. As freshmen, we were excited and scared. Would our moms be cool? What would we do all weekend? Would they buy us beer? How on earth would we sneak away for a smoke?

Friday night, Bridgett was in a play, and afterward we convinced the moms to buy some beer to go with our fancy snacks. Cheese and crackers, some sliced salami, and a veggie tray were all part of the spread. No tortilla chips covered in processed cheese dust or uncooked baked goods for our wonderful mothers. Truthfully, they could have had whatever they wanted. They were buying.

We took the adult food and adult beverages back to our dorm room and got comfortable. As comfortable as three 18-year-olds and their mothers can get sitting on the floor, making small talk. My mom and Kate's mom knew each other, but not well, and we were all just meeting Bridgett's mom. We had been in college for eight months, and our mothers were seeing us in our own "home" for the first time. Never mind that this was a home they paid for, and was the size of a large closet with two desks and a set of bunk beds. It was a bit surreal, but also fun, light, and wonderful. Just a bunch of women, having a good time. My very first grown-up girls' night.

After several hours of dorm room partying with our moms, Bridgett, who had recently reconciled with her high school boyfriend, leaned over and declared, "Buddy. I'm out of The Club." I paused. The club? Oh! The Club! I smirked, and shot back, "Buddy. My mom knows about The Club." I have always been an open book, and I can't resist telling a funny story, even if it's to my mom. Even if it's about hummers. For the record, my mom does not find this trait charming, and she wishes I had more of a filter.

In this moment though, she was entertained. My mom and I started laughing that silent, chest-clutching laugh, while Bridgett turned an impressive shade of scarlet. Kate watched alternating between horror and amusement, and the other two moms looked on, confused. We eventually got everyone calmed down enough to explain what the ABC Club was, and all three of the moms decided our little club was ridiculous and gross. Gross? I was seriously annoyed. They should have been happy their daughters had taken a stand against playing the skin flute, instead of thinking we were silly little college girls. As it turns out, we *were* silly. We didn't even recognize the redundancy of the "C" in ABC Club. Anti-Blowjob Club Club?

We needed some air, and were feeling cramped in the tiny box that was our dorm room, so we all took a 2 a.m. stroll through campus. While Bridgett and her mom discussed The Birds and The Bees: College Edition, my mom and I held hands, Kate and her mom chatted quietly, all six of us reveling in the magic of the first flakes of an April snowstorm. It was a truly special night, beginning with three friends, and ending with three families.

We finally got the moms to bed (which began my Mom's Weekend tradition of trying to tuck my mom in long before she's ready) and we were able to sneak that cigarette. While we walked to Denny's. At 4 a.m. In the snow.

My friends and I *are* "quite the threesome." It began with dorm living, it survived the rest of college when we spent much of our time with different people and living in different places, and it has witnessed nearly 20 years' worth of life. We have helped each other mourn loved ones, proudly stood by and watched each other marry wonderful men (thank the good Lord we all finally got some smarts when it came to choosing partners) and now, despite a gulfing span of 5000 miles keeping us apart, we are honored with Godparent responsibilities and are as connected as we've ever been.

And for the record, we've officially disbanded The ABC Club, much to our husbands' relief.

*Amy and her husband made two kids: a four-year-old girl and a six-year-old boy. She does not consider herself a housewife, as she owns no pearls and only one apron. Amy has been featured on* BlogHer, Aiming Low, Mamapedia, Scary Mommy, *and* Bonbon Break, *and is a contributor to the best-selling book,* I Just Want to Pee Alone. *You can find her laughing at the absurdity of parenting on Facebook and Twitter @FunnyIsFamily, and pinning things she'll never do on Pinterest. She writes embarrassing stories about herself and her family at* FunnyIsFamily.com.

# Oral Hygiene in the Wild, Wild West

*by Allison Hart*

I always carry dental floss with me. *Always.*

For some reason food gets stuck in my teeth every single time I eat. You can't tell from looking at me, but my teeth are perfectly shaped and spaced to trap black, green, and occasionally red remnants of all snacks and meals. These are never easily extracted with a tongue or swish of water. This shit needs floss. While other women quietly excuse themselves immediately after meals to politely reapply lipstick, or impolitely puke up their dinners, I dart for the ladies' room to floss.

When I don't have any floss with me, which happens all too often for someone who always carries some, I improvise. Best alternative? Earrings. (What? Just me?)

Central teeth are relatively easy. I've picked food out of them with items as unlikely as paper folded into a just-stiff-enough but not-too-thick point. It's the back teeth that will give you problems.

If I've got something wedged in the back that an earring can't relieve, until I get my hands on some floss I will desperately try to get it out with anything within reach. Once in a while I get lucky—photographs sometimes work—but often I compound the problem, ending up with a bit of asparagus *and* a bit of book jacket jammed in there.

It was after lunch on one of these unfortunate days when I found myself facing the CEO of my hip "dotcom" company in the ladies' room. The look on her face—confusion, shock, abject terror and revulsion—coupled with my simple yet totally situationally inadequate explanation, *"Flossing,"* still makes me cringe nearly 15 years later.

A little background:

In 1999 San Francisco was filled with (mostly empty) promise. At that time the Internet was the new Wild West. Compensation in stock shares (with no present value) was the norm and seemed reasonable. We were modern-day prospectors and cashing in those shares was as seductive and likely as cashing in gold bullion was to our predecessors. Young, starry-eyed, corporate neophytes like me worked at the countless emerging Internet startups for little pay and the possibility of untold riches. It was short-term sacrifice but the anticipated payoff was worth it—we were *building something*. We didn't say we worked at an Internet startup. We said we worked at a *dotcom*. We were smart, on trend, and about to be millionaires.

This was a brave new world powered by the limitless possibility of the Internet, driven by a new breed of young executives, and backed by entrepreneurs who threw money at these ventures with unquestioning confidence. Outdated concepts of workplaces were chucked for the whims of this new generation of future success stories. Open floor plans replaced corner offices and cubicles. Senior management fraternized with and sat amongst lowly customer service reps. My company even had an indoor

Astroturf dog park so employees could bring their pets to work (a truly terrible idea), where senior management ferrets traded ass sniffs with lowly customer service dogs.

The CEO of my dotcom was a woman all of 28. Two of her business school friends rounded out the management team as the COO and CFO. Their carefully-thought-out and very expensive mimicry of the laid back, anything goes, casual workplace look of the time left the rest of us breathless in their beautiful, designer, well-coiffed wakes. Their concept of the classless office environment left the rest of us stuttering stupidly as we acted unintimidated and feigned nonchalance while chatting with them over the complimentary organic daily "brain food" available in the break room.

I paint this full picture so you can understand what a normal bathroom encounter with my CEO, under the best of normal bathroom circumstances, would be like. In her presence I'd immediately go from my confident, 23-year-old self to a girl with her skirt tucked into her underwear, blurting out weird things about ferrets and dogs and ass sniffing. But this was not a normal bathroom encounter under normal bathroom circumstances.

On that fateful and embarrassing day, I believe the culprit was a burrito. Black beans, beef, wilted shredded lettuce . . . ugh. Talk about a variety of potential dental lodgers! No floss. No toothpicks. No earrings! I slipped the straw from my drink into my purse. Once safely in the bathroom back at the office, some creative straw application ought to do the trick.

It did not do the trick.

I tried both ends until they were bent and useless. Stupid straw. I dug through my purse. A business card! Instead of getting the food *out*, a corner of the card stayed *in*. I was going in the wrong direction. I had nothing else to use. I looked at myself in the mirror.

My hair?

No. It hadn't come to that. Not *that*.

And then I spied the perfect floss replacement. It had been right in front of me the whole time. For years in fact. Often right in my purse. On the vanity beside the sink was a lovely basket full of complimentary tampons. What do tampons have if not a braid of (admittedly rustic) floss?

I tore into one and unraveled the string until I got a strand that was both thin and strong enough. This was going to work! I felt exuberant as I assumed the position, cupping the business end of the tampon in my right hand and holding taut the end of my slightly yarnish floss in my left. (If you've never had a piece of a business card rammed between your molars, you may not understand the passion I felt at its imminent release.) With a firm upward push, I got the "floss" between the offending teeth.

At that moment the door opened.

In walked the incredibly cool, successful, beautiful, intimidating, rich, smart, idolized CEO. With cat-like reflexes I dropped my hands, adopting a casual, "just hanging in the bathroom" demeanor. Nothing weird going on here. I smiled at her. She stopped in her tracks, *staring*, her response to my "Oh! Hi!" apparently caught in her throat.

Then I felt something sort of brushing the side of my chin. A quick glance to the mirror explained everything (to *me*).

I had a tampon hanging out of my mouth.

Because I put a tampon string between my teeth.

And left it there. Dangling.

O. M. G.

"*Flossing*," I said. As if that explained anything.

She moved quickly past me, averting her eyes.

I spent the rest of my employment there humiliated, with the sound of "*Flossing*" echoing in my head.

Since then I always carry floss. *Always.* Well, at least I *always* wear earrings . . . most of the time.

*Allison Hart writes the humorous and (sometimes brutally) honest blog* Motherhood, WTF? *Her tagline is: "I'm the mom who makes you feel better about your parenting." She does this by saying the things that other moms have the good sense to only think.* Motherhood, WTF? *has received numerous awards and accolades over the years in Allison's imagination. In real life, it was listed by* Babble *as one of the Top 100 Mom Blogs of 2012 and by* Circle of Moms *as a Top 25 Humor Mom Blog in both 2011 and 2012. Allison's work has been featured on* BlogHer, In The Powder Room, *and* Scary Mommy. *When not banging her head against the wall and repeating herself to her children, she can be found on Facebook and Twitter @motherhoodwtf.*

# Act Like You've Got Sense...
# Like a Mafia Don

*by Suniverse*

You want to be considered a professional? You'll have to act like one.

What's that, Sally? You can't believe that something you wrote in a secret Facebook group thread got out to the public and it's making you look bad?

Come on, Johnny, you're stunned that the sexts you sent your office crush were found by her husband and now you're both in a world of hurt?

And Jane. Really? Drunk Instagrams of you and . . . whoever that was with the python around his neck . . . ended up trending on #DrunkWhoresOfTwitter and you're surprised that your boss is a little pissed?

Your reputation is important. It's the foundation for everything you do. And if you can't keep it together enough to keep from looking like an asshole, you need help. As a society, we need to stop acting like morons with zero understanding of technology. Your actions speak louder than your words. If you act like a dummy, you're going to get called out. If you act unprofessionally, people are going to think twice about dealing with you. While most people would recommend reading books by or about icons of business to guide your professional behavior, I recommend fashioning yourself after some true professionals—those leaders of what was once called the Family Business: Mafia Dons.

Not so much with the killing and drug dealing and gambling and prostitution, but in the way they take care of business and protect their reputations. Mafia Dons know what's what. They know that image is everything. If you behave like a shmuck, you're going to get whacked. So Mafia Dons protect their images. They take care to keep their names unsullied. They know who their confidants are, and trust the right people. They understand that their words may be used against them, and take care when they speak.

Mafia Dons also understand that reputation is everything. Mr. John Gotti, for example, was known as "The Teflon Don," because nothing the government threw at him stuck. Sure, he may have used physical intimidation to keep his name from being besmirched, but he was also smart enough to understand that this was not his only option. He protected his reputation by discussing his business in a business-like manner.

Other Mafia Dons take care to cultivate their professional demeanors. They know that they are being watched, and that their actions and activities are reviewed under a microscope. As a professional, you should give the same thoughtful care to your actions.

Wondering what steps to take to cement your standing as someone who can be counted on in a pinch? Here you go:

**1. Assume every phone call is being recorded.** Think about what you're saying. We all need bitch sessions—I am guilty of calling a friend solely to complain about something—but think about whether you'd be comfortable knowing your shit talk was broadcast for everyone to hear. Mafia Dons know that the government is always trying to catch them saying something incriminating on a wire tap, and so they tailor their speech. If you're interested in being treated like a professional, act like one when you're discussing your work, always.

**2. Assume every email and text is being forwarded.** We've all found ourselves accidentally sending the dreaded Reply All. If we're lucky, it's an innocuous response. If we're not, then it's a conflagration and everyone has a ringside seat. Sexting? Sure, so long as you don't mind your grandma reading that stuff. I'm married and I still feel awkward when the husband and I text each other anything that has to do with sex. When you're a professional, you need to keep your work email and phone professional. Save the other stuff for your *Yahoo!* account.

**3. Everyone gets a nickname.** Everyone. This way, you know who you're discussing, but people who overhear you or accidently read a misdirected text aren't sure who you're talking about. I'd suggest being more creative with nicknames than the standard *Sopranos*-type nomenclature of Big Paulie, Little Paulie, etc. Showcase your creativity—it's your time to shine!

**4. Be clear in your work.** A Mafia Don takes care to be sure that his or her message gets to the intended recipient and is clearly stated, sometimes with brutal emphasis. When you offer your work to the world, you want to make sure your point is understandable. You also want to make sure that you're not lost in a lot of nattering—think outside the box and tackle topics that aren't done to death.

**5. Casual Friday does not mean wear clothes from Love Pink or whatever that terrible store is.** The rise of the casual workplace has created more minefields for women than for men. Sucks, but it's true. Mafia Dons know that how you look conveys worlds about you and your standing. Mr. Gotti, for example, was always dressed impeccably, because he knew that how he looked carried weight. No one is ever going to think, "Why is she wearing a suit?" at your job and think less of you, but they will think, "Is it pajama day?" if you show up wearing a hoodie. Err on the side of conservative professionalism. Enjoy your flip-flops at home.

Take my advice, and the cannoli, and you'll soon be making people offers they can't refuse. Act like a professional, and you'll be treated with the respect you so richly deserve. Cement your standing in your community by acting like a stand-up guy, and there's very little chance you'll end up with a horse's head in your bed. You'll soon have a professional reputation that will precede you, and keep you out of prison. Probably.

*Suniverse has spent lo these many years perfecting her use of swears and snarking in the third person. She's written for* In the Powder Room, Funny not Slutty, Aiming Low, *and* Studio 30 Plus. *You can find her waxing rhapsodic with four-letter words at her blog,* The Suniverse, *on Twitter @TheSuniverse, and keeping a low profile on Facebook. She denies taking part in TP-ing your house.*

# My Vagina Is Like a Flower—a Cauliflower

*by Lady Estrogen*

We all have friends who fill various positions and/or needs in our lives. In my experience, whether completely by accident or formed by my diabolical subconscious mind, my friends could fill a rainbow of differences with their admirable qualities. It's like I'm a goddamn Rotary Club . . . except without the erectile dysfunction.

I'm sure the friendships we make in our college years are quite different from those we've had since childhood, particularly in the over-share department. I have had the same BFF since I was seven-years-old, but there are things I wouldn't even remotely consider discussing with her—whereas with friends I've made later in life, I wouldn't even bat a single mascara-smeared eyelash.

My closest friend from college actually managed to survive living with me; not many females can make that claim, that's for sure. What is it with living with multiple females that makes us all lose our fucking minds? Anyway, I digress.

Apart from that one time when we made out for the sole purpose of turning on the lumps of drunken testosterone in the room (and no butterflies went off in my stomach), we are, and always have been 100% platonic (despite my bisexual track record). We do, however, discuss our sex lives and experiences...at great lengths. If talking about all the gory details of sexual misadventures was a sport likened to doubles tennis, we'd be the bloody champions.

Fast-forward a few years and the, umm, *natural* progression from constantly talking about sex would be that of pregnancy, I guess. My friend was macabrely fascinated by my pregnancy with my twins, not only because they were twins, but also because the very idea of growing ANY number of humans inside our bodies is a concept she finds disturbing and gross. Some of us are born with the motherhood gene and some of us are definitely not; she is one of the latter. That still never stopped her from asking highly intimate questions about the changes my body was going through, if for no other reason than to respond to my stories consistently with an "Ewww!"

Months had slowly passed with my multiples pregnancy and finally I had come to a point where I was wearing a support belt to hold up my stomach for fear that it would simply rip off my body from all the weight. I hadn't seen my toes in at least three months and my vagina for even longer. Dammit! Even the "hold a mirror under my crotch" technique didn't work, but nevertheless, I knew something was going on down there—I could feel it, barely.

My dear friend had come over for a long-overdue visit (no pun intended) and after our initial catching up, I broke into the gory details.

"Something is wrong with my vagina."

"What do you mean, wrong? Like, a yeast infection or something?"

"No. It just feels weird."

"Weird?"

"Yeah, weird. Like a giant bearded prune, weird."

"Ewww. Gross! What's happening to it?!"

"I don't know. Maybe the weight from my stomach is smooshing it all up or something?"

"I wanna see it!"

"Seriously?"

"Hell yeah. For purely scientific purposes, obviously."

"Obviously."

"C'mon. Peel off those stretchy pants of yours and let me check out your snatch!"

"Classy."

"What? I'm sure if I was a Gyno and I said that, I'd be a hit with all my patients."

"Ha. I'm sure you would."

And I then proceeded to take off my pants and giant underwear that would put "granny panties" to shame. I kept my belly belt on as I hiked my right leg up onto the edge of the bathtub. My friend's eyes widened as she took a long, laboured breath, as if she was about to go deep sea diving . . . but with my vagina. She slowly knelt down to assume the position of inspection. I felt good about it. *Ahem.*

"You sure you're OK with looking at my fucked up lady bits?"

"Yeah. It's too late to turn back now! I've just GOT to see it. You OK?"

"I guess."

About five of the longest seconds of my life went by while she had one hand leaning on my monstrous stomach and her head cocked to the left and angled right all up in my business . . . then she emerged.

"Holy hell. I'm sooooo sorry!"

"WHAT?! What is it? What's wrong with my bits?"

"It looks like a cauliflower . . . or a 120-year-old woman trying to smile."

"What. The. Fuck?"

"I'm just trying to describe what I saw. Did you want me to take a photo for you with your cell phone?"

"HHHH-HELL NO. I DO NOT NEED PHOTOGRAPHIC EVIDENCE OF THIS, THANKS."

"So, I think you're right. It's gotta be a gravity thing or something like that. For your sake, and your husband's, I hope it goes back to normal after you have the twins!"

"Yes, I'm hoping for that too! I'm a bit devastated right now."

"It is fairly disgusting."

"You always know *just* what to say."

"LLLLL-love you . . . now put your pants back on. It's just getting to be too much."

"Well, I might as well drop a deuce while I'm here. Undressing is a lot of effort these days, ya know."

"Fantastic. I'll be out having a smoke, trying to erase what I've just witnessed."

"Just you wait! I'll be showing you my C-section staples before not too long!"

"Oh my fucking God. I'm NEVER having a baby."

This is pretty much a perfect illustration of one of my most highly valued and cherished friendships. Perhaps the fact that she had gazed upon my cauliflorous vagina and survived with minimal emotional scarring has made our friendship all-the-closer for it.

And I wouldn't trade it for the world.

Although, I have to admit, I have never been able to eat cauliflower since, particularly with my grandmother's affection for smothering it with Velveeta cheese sauce.

*Lady Estrogen is a work from home mom with 2.5 kids from Toronto'ish, Canada. She is a communications and creative media director and uses her zero bullshit attitude in her work, sex life, and as a mother. It doesn't always go over very well, but she's also used to getting into trouble. You can find her ranting and swearing on Twitter about any given topic @ladyestrogen, and her highly enlightening, slightly vibrating, yet occasionally neglected blog can be found at www.ladye.me.*

# Second Husband Material

*by Amy Wruble*

John would have made a great second husband. Unfortunately I was 23, and not even close to being ready for a first husband. I met him at the ad agency where we both worked, in New York. He grew on me slowly, like a developing Polaroid. The final picture was smart and serious, with floppy hair, soulful blue eyes and a lanky body draped in skinny neckties. Our connection was real, but it was geography that fast-tracked our flirting into a relationship. John lived way out in Hoboken, and my Manhattan studio was a quick F train ride to the office. Get your mind out of the gutter—it really was the F train.

At first, I loved being with John—loved the security of his certainty. He wanted me and only me. We could literally talk for hours, holding hands across the table in candlelit restaurants, drinking wine and flexing our East Coast wit with rapid-fire banter, my Rosalind Russell to his Cary Grant. John was just a year older than me, but far more mature. He loved theater, classic films and *The New York Times*. So did I. But he hated crowds and bars and parties. That's where we differed. I was just two years out of college and still craving adventure and drama. John had a hot young body but a middle-aged brain. I started thinking that he would make a great second husband—you know, the one you sip iced tea with on the porch swing, easing contentedly into your golden years, grateful to have survived your exciting but no-good first husband who long ago skipped town, leaving you with his gambling debts. I wanted to keep John on ice for ten years. Maybe 20.

Another "con" (on the list I was always mentally composing, never a good sign) was that John became intensely jealous when other men looked at me or I looked at other men. The more he accused me of making flirty eyes at strangers, the more I felt compelled to do it, like a child unable to resist poking an electrical outlet with a fork. He complained that my outfits were too provocative. One time, we were getting ready for disco night (my suggestion) at a Chelsea gay bar. I wanted to play dress up, but John insisted I change out of my bustier and hot pants. He called me Heidi Ho—like it was a bad thing. I started to feel like I was dating my dad.

Nope, I didn't like John telling me what to wear or whom to ogle. And I wanted to dance in hot pants. Feeling claustrophobic, I broke it off. Maybe we just needed time apart and then I'd feel less suffocated and welcome him back. I knew separating was a risky move; John was definitely a catch—handsome, smart and kind. Other women would want him. Why didn't I? The Rolling Stones say, "You can't always get what you want." In my case, it was "You can't always want what you get."

A few nights alone and I did start to miss him, though not enough to actually pick up the phone and do something about it. I was so wrapped up in *my* choices and *my* needs that I gave no thought to what John might be doing or thinking without me. So I was understandably shocked when just three weeks later, the office was buzzing with news that John had gotten engaged to his high school sweetheart. It was crazy how fast he'd moved. In the three weeks since we'd broken up, he'd reunited with his ex, procured an engagement ring, traveled upstate to ask her father for her hand, planned a romantic proposal scenario, gotten engaged, and thoroughly freaked me out. What had I done in the past three weeks? Not even the laundry.

I skipped over sad and went straight to psycho. Hell hath no fury like a woman who doesn't want her boyfriend until somebody else does. I became single-mindedly obsessed with winning John back. He had been mine just weeks ago—surely I could make him mine again. But how? Rosalind Russell was no good to me now. I needed Barbara Stanwyck. Smokey eyes, side part, withering stare. Mentally and physically, I made myself over as a *femme fatale*, stopping just short of taking up smoking.

After some light surveillance to ensure that John was both home and alone, I showed up at his Hoboken doorstep late one night, unannounced, in nothing but a trench coat and heels. Truth be told, he was less surprised to find his ex in a raincoat than he was to see that I'd actually crossed the river to New Jersey, something I'd never agreed to do when we were dating.

So there I was, vamping it up as I dropped my coat, wishing he had Venetian blinds so they'd cast striped *film noir* shadows on my body, but making do with available lighting. I told him I missed him so much. I let my eyes mist up just a little. (This was easy. My pointy stilettos were killing me.) And then I gave him "The Look."

Did he sleep with me? Of course he did. Did it change anything? Of course it didn't.

In the morning, he was still engaged and I was the jackass who had to take the PATH train back into Manhattan in a raincoat and fuck-me pumps on a beautiful sunny day. I actually hoped the people on the train thought I was a stripper on her way to an office bachelor party, which would be far more dignified than my reality.

It was pretty awkward at work after that, but then John changed jobs and I got to stop hiding behind the Xerox. For a few years after I lost my second husband to his first wife, I wondered if he was the one that got away. But thinking back on all the adventures I couldn't have had and the mistakes I wouldn't have made, it's hard to imagine doing it any differently.

My fiancé would probably agree.

*Amy Wruble is a writer and toddler mom who works from home, where she is carrying on a scandalous inter-office romance with the Jolly Green Giant. She blogs at* Carriage Before Marriage *and also writes for* The Huffington Post, Babytalk, Parenting, Lifetime Moms, In The Powder Room, *and* Families in the Loop. *Please connect with her on Twitter @Cb4M and Facebook (Carriage Before Marriage), her only adult social outlets.*

## Confucius Say: When Shit Hits Fan, Girlfriends Bring Pooper Scooper

*by Janie Emaus*

What my husband told me when I was eight and a half months pregnant almost caused me to give birth on the sticky vinyl seat in our favorite Chinese restaurant. With the fortune cookie crushed between my fingers, I leaned forward and threw his words back to him in question form.

"You're getting laid off? And you didn't have a clue?"

He nodded. "It's a good time to start my own business, don't you think?"

A good time? Didn't he know we were about to have a baby? (Who at that very moment was doing somersaults in rhythm with my heartbeats).

"Well?" he shrugged.

And as his shoulders dropped, so did my dream of being a stay-at-home mom. After all, one of us had to bring in a steady income.

Trying to remain calm, I cracked open my cookie and pulled out the fortune.

*The light at the end of the tunnel may be an oncoming train.*

WTF? Was this for real?

Well, the reality was—my future may have just taken a U-turn, but I'd be damned if it was going to get run over.

As the tears ran down my husband's face, I reached across the table for his hand and promised him that everything was going to be OK.

And then I turned to the people who knew me best: my girlfriends.

By this time in our lives, our early 30s, I'd known most of them for over 15 years. Even though they were all dealing with issues of their own—new babies, sore nipples, pre-school decisions, infertility—they listened to my problem. We talked. We walked. We drank cheap wine. We cried and laughed.

And time went by.

Fast-forward ten years.

Once again, I sat across from my husband in the same Chinese restaurant. After several moments of awkward silence, he leaned forward and announced that my 16-year-old stepson was leaving us to live with his mother.

"I didn't even know he was thinking of doing this," my husband said, burying his head in his hands.

He couldn't be that clueless, could he? Not if he actually knew his son, or life for that matter.

Isn't it always greener on the other side of the fence? That is, until you get there and smell the same old fertilizer.

I reached across the table, took his hand and promised him we'd get through this. It would all turn out OK.

And then I turned to those who knew me best: my girlfriends.

By this time, we were in our late 40s. Gone were the diapers, midnight feedings and those horrible *Mommy and Me* classes where everyone pretended to be having a great time, but couldn't wait for it to end. Now we dealt with teenage aliens, divorces and financial gurus promising to make us fortunes by the time we reached the half-century mark.

But, as always, my girlfriends took time to listen to my story and help me through the situation.

We talked and walked. We drank cosmopolitans. We cried. We laughed.

And time went by.

Until just a few months ago, when my husband told me something that changed our lives forever.

He was diagnosed with a brain tumor. Not a small one, mind you. But one that was sticking out of the top of his head, like a golf ball.

I stared at him incredulously. How could he not know something *that* large was growing on his body? Didn't he have a clue? As women, we're always checking ourselves, feeling for lumps and bumps. Any little unwanted protrusion and we're off to the doctor to have it examined.

I did feel a bit guilty for not noticing it myself. But, really how often do you rub the top of your husband's head?

Granted, we still have sex. But after 34 years of marriage, it's more of the relaxed kind than the "rail-grabbing, hanging-off-the-bedside, hair-pulling" type of our early years together. To be truly honest, sometimes, I look at the clock wondering if we'll be done before *The Voice* starts. Or I'm making lists of things that need to get done around the house.

So, after the initial shock, we faced the situation head on. Together. And I mean, *together*.

I became the designated driver. He became the "pain in the neck" passenger.

He went through the eight-hour surgery, unaware of anything. I went through it, aware of *everything*. The skid marks on the hospital floor. The buzzing of the overhead lights. The chipped nail on my left thumb.

After his surgery, we spent four lovely nights together in the ICU. By night number three, I almost figured out how to climb onto my folding recliner without getting my foot caught between the cushions. The casino-sounding beeps and dings emanating from the nurses' station became the soundtrack for my dreams.

The cafeteria guy snuck me a cup of coffee each morning. I snuck sips of vodka from a flask each night.

I held my breath every hour when the nurse would come to check my husband's vitals. Knowing it was vitally important for him to get out of the hospital before we killed each other with so much togetherness.

And through it all, I turned to my girlfriends.

Now in the second half of our lives, with grandchildren, aging parents and retirement doubts (thanks to those so-called gurus) we walked and talked and met for quiet dinners, drinking extra-cold, extra-dry martinis.

As always, I couldn't have gotten through this without them. They were the super glue that held me together.

Several weeks ago, with the tumor behind us, my husband and I went to our Chinese restaurant.

This time when I opened up my fortune cookie, I found it empty.

"Well, I guess I don't have a future," I said, holding my hands in the air.

"Not so." My husband set his cookie on the table between us, grabbed my hand and pressed it up against his heart. "You can share mine. Besides, isn't that what we've been doing all along?"

I guess he is not so clueless after all.

*Janie Emaus is the author of the time travel romance,* Before the After, *and the young adult novel,* Mercury in Retro Love. *She is a staff writer at* In The Powder Room *and blogs frequently for* The Huffington Post, Better After 50, *and* Generation Fabulous. *She is proud to be named a 2013* BlogHer Voice of the Year. *Janie believes that when the world is falling apart, we're just one laugh away from putting it together again. To learn more about Janie visit her blog* TheBoomerRants.com *and her website* JanieEmaus.com. *You can connect with her on Facebook and Twitter @Janie5010.*

# I Have a Dress Problem

*by Meredith Spidel*

"I have a dress-ordering problem," I told my sister via our nightly phone call.

She sighed. "What do you mean?" *This should have been my first indication that I was questionably sane.*

"I started ordering dresses and I can't stop. Should I look for a support group?"

"This isn't a thing. It doesn't happen in real life."

"It happens in my life."

Another sigh. "Tell me."

"I had to buy a swimsuit. I haven't bought a new one in seven years." *What is this jazz about hipster bikinis, anyway?*

"Of course." *She really meant "Holy crap, my sister is crazy, and I'm going to be admitting her to the psychiatric hospital."*

"I logged onto Lands' End."

"Oh for the love of God . . ." The defeat in her voice was palpable. *Read: Sorry, Lands' End is for "grown" women. You have officially crossed over, and now I'm scared.*

"To get the free shipping, I had to spend $75. So I started browsing, and this is when it all went sour. I remembered I needed a cute dress for this summer."

"Sure."

"They have A LOT of cool stuff! Seriously, listen, this is so not 2011. Lands' End has completely stepped up their game." *I could hear through her breathing patterns that there was no chance on God's green earth she would believe Lands' End sold anything slightly more modern than what my grandma bought through her local old-lady dress shop in the '80s.*

"And?"

"*And*, I bought a 'few' because I couldn't decide on one. Plus, they have free returns at Sears, so I could just take back the ones I couldn't squeeze my hips into."

"I feel like there is more to this story."

"Well, a friend reminded me that, as a mom, I really need some t-shirt dresses for playing with the kids this summer, so I went to Old Navy and . . ." *If you buy in bulk, it really is cheaper.*

"Mmmhh?" my sister braced herself for the continuance of my extreme logic.

"Well, you know I like to shop around for the best deal, and I found out Target had some nice ones too. I only needed to spend $50 to get 20% off! Also, I needed sandals."

"Have you told Jared?"

"Listen, I'm trying to keep this on the DL until I can return a few of the dresses." *My husband is more a fan of saving money than spending money. He's just so old-school like that.*

"A FEW?! How many do you have?"

"Enough . . . but I'm being extremely economical and savvy because I *did* pass on the gorgeous $126 dress I saw at LOFT. I had to get some new Spanx though. They're so expensive. Like $44 expensive. Also, I had to get my nails done because we are going on a business trip for Jared's work. And obviously I needed a pedi and there may have been an accidental first-time lip wax...do you think I need a new purse?" *I was sure everyone at the conference would be looking at nothing but my nails. Also, it makes me want to shoot myself a little that I now need Spanx to look non-whale in a dress. Yes, hate on 17-year-olds just a little because their bums are just so darn perky.*

Silence as she debated whether there was any way to break the biological bond that ties us. "Do you have any friends close to you who might like to help you with this situation?"

*What in the world did she mean, "Do I have any friends close to me?" YOU CANNOT SHIRK YOUR SISTERLY DUTY!*

I laid it on the line, "This is your responsibility. You are going to have to come here and sort through these dresses and figure out what I should return."

"You can't do this yourself?"

"It doesn't make sense any more. I tried sorting them and I got confused. I don't know what I should keep any more."

"You are annoying me."

"I am annoying myself."

"How many dresses are there?"

"I don't want to talk about this right now."

The irritating little chick would not be deterred, "How many dresses are there?"

"I had to stash a small pile under my bed so Jared doesn't figure it out."

"Tell me."

"Are you including skirts in this number? I also got a couple pairs of adorable shorts."

"Tell me."

"Sixteen."

"SIXTEEN!?"

"Sixteen."

"You do realize that people get divorced, right?"

"Screw you. I said I had a dress-ordering problem. Not a creepin'-with-random-guys-while-my-kids-are-at-soccer-practice meth addiction." *Do you think my husband really would leave me over the dress situation? Wasn't the fact that I birthed his children sort of insurance against little events like this causing a rift?*

"I give up. Where does this knowledge of meth-addicted soccer moms come from?"

"I saw it on Oprah."

"I have no idea what to say at this point."

"I know. I still love you."

"I'm not sure I can say that back right now. What are you doing about the dresses?"

I paused, grasping to secure a reasonable and sensible solution, "If I paid someone to come watch my kids so I could spend the day returning this crapload of dresses do you think it would even out?"

"You still spent the money upfront, so . . . no."

*Dead silence as we waited for some unknown force to miraculously remedy the seemingly hopeless irresponsible spending situation. As it turned out, God is smart, and classy, and just wasn't going to play my silly dress games. I was on my own.*

I reminded my sister, "If Jared and I die, you are getting my children, you know."

"How is this helpful right now?"

"It's not. I'm just sort of bitter toward you right now and wanted to throw that in your face because I'm grouchy. Also, I'm jealous that you are twenty-six, don't have kids, and have time to mulch your lawn. And Elyse needs her diaper changed more than four times a day, so you'll have that to deal with if I'm dead."

"Listen, you are the one with the problem."

"EXACTLY. I have a Dress. Ordering. Problem. Fix it. Please."

"How many dresses do you actually need this summer?" *What the heck, Judas?! Why was she bringing up irrelevant points like what I actually needed or didn't need? I always knew she had it in for me.*

"Whatever, ho. Your lack of empathy totally sucks, by the way."

"You are the one buying cases of t-shirt dresses that you can't afford and you're mad at me?"

"Exactly." *I love her, but she was being so irrational that it was becoming hurtful.*

"Whatever. I need to go make dinner." SELL-OUT.

"This is not an end to this discussion. You still need to come here and sort my dresses." I was serious.

"What time should we be there on Saturday?" *What the what? I was in crisis mode here and she was talking about a freakin' family barbeque! Get on board, sister.*

"I AM HAVING A PROBLEM."

"Sure. Should I bring the potato salad?"

"I hate you."

"I know."

*Meredith blogs at TheMomOfTheYear.net, dedicatedly earning her title one epic parenting fail at a time. When her kids aren't busy pummeling each other with Legos or requiring their 16th sippy cup refill of the day, she tries to offer quick, relatable laughs for fellow parents of the world and all their empathizers. She remains entirely terrified by crafts, promises to never share any useful household tips, and is fully committed to a less serious look at the world of parenting. Social media is beyond her comprehension, but she makes a pass at Twitter @MeredithSpidel and Facebook (TheMomOfTheYear).*

# Then I Asked: What Should I Know About Having a Kid?

*by Kim Bongiorno*

"Hey, Melissa—is there anything I should know about having this kid that isn't in the books I've been reading?"

Sunlight streamed through the window, making the golden, hormone-induced mutton chops glisten upon my cheeks. As I waited for her answer, I thumbed through the glossy parenting magazines on her kitchen table.

A candle flickered by the sink, adding sweetness to the spit-up scented air that was getting punched in the face by a diaper change. My immensely pregnant belly cast a shadow over my friend as she squatted on the floor, pinning a pungent, wiggly 11-month-old down with her knee in an attempt to wipe stew-like poo from his bitty boy parts.

Melissa snapped the last diaper tab in place, released her boy, and turned to meet my eye. "What do you mean, 'anything'?"

I gestured to my soon-to-be-firstborn-baby bump and then to the motherhood shrapnel surrounding us on every surface of the room. "The stuff that isn't pretty. All of it."

She looked at me like a murderess about to confess a truth from which the witness may never recover. "All of it?"

"Yes."

She nodded and turned on her heel, a sweep of tangled hair that hadn't seen a brush in days trailing behind her. There was some rustling around in her bedroom; she bolted back out and ordered me to sit.

I waddled over to the once-white couch and plopped onto the crunchy cushions.

Melissa had the posture of someone about to give a great speech—I tried to keep my mouth breathing as quiet as possible. Could I make it another five minutes without peeing?

She pushed aside a teething ring, *Baby Einstein* DVD, and burp cloth to lay down a well-worn stack of treasured Post-its.

Then she jumped right into telling me *everything* I needed to know about labor, childbirth, post-delivery, newborns, and life as a new parent, as outlined on the Post-its she bestowed on me, as someone had once done for her. Not the shiny, happy lies that we see on diaper commercials, but the things only close girlfriends can say without softening the edges with bullshit.

Now, I love lists. So every aspect of this new parenting adventure felt under control because I had a list for each of them: hospital bag, birth plan, nursery supplies—all of it. Melissa laughed at my well-intentioned lists and metaphorically threw them in the still-steamy diaper pail.

Since that day I've had two kids, and I can say whole-heartedly: she was right about everything.

Listing "I want calm music and a pleasant object to focus on" pretty much guarantees you'll deliver in a taxi during rush hour. Babies decide how they want to come out, your carefully packed hospital bag be damned. All you really need is your insurance card, socks, a cold can of Dermoplast Pain Relieving Spray for your crotch, and an empty bag to lug supplies you'll steal from the nurses' station when you're sent home.

Labor will hurt like hell, and you will say terrible things to people you love. Oddly enough, you'll be more pleasant to the total strangers in the room. Like the anesthesiologist. If he manages a perfect epidural, he'll end up in your will before you can say "I LOVE THIS GUY SO MUCH."

Think carefully about whether you want to have a mirror in front of your pulsating honey pot, because someone will ask you if you want to watch your delivery. This seems cool before you realize you'll witness cottage cheese, beach foam, refried beans, watered-down Jell-O, and more squirty DNA than you ever thought one person could contain, rush out of your vagina before the kid does. We don't have uteruses; we have really wet clown cars.

Once baby arrives, a nurse will wipe him off, place him on your chest, and you will be in shock at how amazing he is already. You will also be a little skeeved at the nasty goo clinging to his back fur, and concerned that his face looks more like your alcoholic ex-boxer Uncle Nick on a bender, than either you or your husband.

Once delivery is over and you are moved to your semi-private room, you'll be ready for some alone time—with a roommate you've never met before and instantly hate. Prepare to take a loud piss eight feet from her bed.

A nurse will escort you into a little bathroom, help you remove giant mesh underwear and blood-soaked maxi pads that stretch from your navel to the top of your butt crack, then watch you

⅃st pee, while aiming a peri bottle of warm water at

⅃rple fist of plums formerly known as your genitals.

⅃elp at the pain of hot urine on fresh stitches, she'll squirt

y⅃          ⅃k like a Super Soaker marksman, which would seem quite odd if it wasn't keeping you from dying while relieving your bladder.

You can't leave the hospital until you've pooped, and that is ten bazillion times worse than the pain of childbirth. After the first post-birth delivery to the porcelain pool, you will decide to never eat solid foods again. Then a cousin will show up with a cheesecake and you will make that entire dessert your bitch in less than two minutes. Then you will cry. Then you will fall asleep right before a nurse needs to wake you up to give you a stool softener.

By the second day after delivering, your boobs will have grown from 36Check-These-Out to 38WTF? Logistically speaking, there is no extra space on your body or in the immediate area surrounding you for them to go, but the milk's gonna come in, so out they will expand. Massive, shiny, veiny, flesh balloons that Pinhead from *Hellraiser* would hang at his retirement party. Then you'll try to feed a baby from them, which is like trying to force a delicate, blind, impatient creature to suck a rock for sustenance: not all too easy.

Sooner than you're ready, your husband will be dropping f-bombs trying to install the car seat in your vehicle while you ponder how to climb in without actually moving, because moving makes your swollen lady parts feel like a cat is trying to claw its way out of them. Then you'll be home, and freaking out because *a hospital just left you in charge of a baby forever.*

That's when you'll start to realize that a pretty nursery is only for photographing and sharing on Facebook. All diapers are actually changed on floors, couches or beds, and your baby is stuck to you like really loud Velcro for a solid 60 days, so just think of a nursery as a huge walk-in closet for tiny clothes and bulk boxes of diapers.

Speaking of which, start saving now for the 60–80 diapers a week you will go through. That's right: 60-80 *a week*. I came down with a case of Carpal Tunnel the first time I heard that. And here's a shocker: the recommended physical therapy for Carpal Tunnel Syndrome does *not* include breastfeeding a starving pterodactyl every 2–3 hours for six weeks straight.

Between feeding the baby and changing his diapers, you will be swaying back and forth. Usually while holding the baby and going "*Shhhhh.*" Sometimes you'll just be holding a sandwich. You'll sway while burping him, while pouring yourself a glass of water, while waiting in line at each of the 17 pediatrician visits you'll go to in the first month. You'll even sway while applying ointment to your burning, chewed-up pumpkin pancake nipples in a dark bathroom.

Then there are the emotions. No, not the "baby blues." It is more like My Sanity Was Delivered With My Placenta. You will be stoic while applying cabbage heads to soothe your mastitis-plagued boobs, then you'll see that the box of Ritz in the cabinet is empty, and go on an hour-long crying jag. You'll love your baby so much that you'll hate your husband for putting mismatched socks on him. Then you'll feel bursts of so much joy that you'll forgive everyone and everything that shredded your vagina, broke your butt, and disabled your sanity to get you here.

\* \* \*

Eight years ago I left Melissa's apartment with a fistful of honesty and permission to not be afraid of imperfection. I went on to have another kid, had my angry plum butt surgically corrected (twice), and began adoring my husband more than the anesthesiologist again. I also typed up that cherished stack of Post-it notes into a document complete with the addition of my own experiences, and shared it freely.

It felt good to have moms-to-be thank me for that document, even though they never failed to ask me one last time after reading it through, "So, Kim, is there anything else you think I should know?"

I'd reply, "It's all in there, and don't worry: by the time they reach the end of infancy, you'll be done with the hardest part of parenting. Just kidding! There's still potty training a terrible two-year-old in your future," and then I'd laugh and laugh . . .

*Kim Bongiorno is an author, freelance writer, and blogger. Best known for hitting with the funny then surprising with the sweet on her blog* Let Me Start By Saying, *she has also been published in three additional books, writes for various websites, was selected as a 2013 BlogHer* Voice of the Year, *and is both a staff writer and the Social Media Manager at* In The Powder Room. *Kim lives in New Jersey with her handsome husband and two charmingly loud kids. Learn more on her author website* Kim Bongiorno Writes *and connect with her on Twitter @LetMeStart.*

# The Adoption Option (and the Idiots Who Try to Talk to You About It)

*by Stephanie Giese*

I am a mom of three. My oldest is adopted and my younger two children are biological. At this stage in our lives it is a non-issue. It is a part of our life that we are happy to discuss, but rarely comes up in casual conversation. This, however, was not the case when we were planning to adopt out of the foster care system back in 2007.

It was something I always had a heart to do and, at age 23, somehow convinced my brand new husband that we should relentlessly pursue. We took the classes, got a home study done and approved, and bada-bing, a year and a half later we had a placement.

We were shocked when our new child came to us at only 13-months-old. We had expected and been prepared for a much older child who would probably look different than we do. Instead we got an adorable toddler with porcelain skin. Most people were polite and complimentary (or so they thought) towards our new little one when they saw him.

"Oh, he's so cute. And you even managed to get a white one."

"He doesn't even look adopted."

"You know, when you first started talking about taking in one of 'those' children, I was concerned. But, just look at him, no one would ever know. He'll just fit right in, won't he?"

Adopted children and wedding dresses, the whiter and smaller the better. So says popular opinion, anyway.

It was my own fault really; I had a newfound sense of pride and altruism on top of my "overwhelmed new mom" aura that left me retelling his whole life story to anyone who would listen. The checkout lady at the grocery store, the other moms at the park, my co-workers, family members, parking lot attendants, anyone who dared to utter an ounce of advice, compassion, or criticism got the whole shebang. Allow me to set the scene:

*The baby is crying in his stroller because he is 13-months-old and that's what they do. I am convinced this is entirely my fault— a direct result of some obvious failure of my own as a rookie mom. In fact, I'm not even comfortable calling myself his "mom" yet because we are still in the awkward limbo phase, meeting with social workers every 30 days before we set our official court date. Try before you buy. That's how the foster care system works.*

Stranger in the checkout line at Target: "Uh-oh, looks like someone needs a nap, huh, Mommy?"

Me: "Do you think so? I'm not really his mommy. I mean, I guess I am. Or I will be soon. Don't worry I didn't kidnap him or anything. Oh gosh, is that something a kidnapper would say? It's just that we are in the process of adopting him. He was in foster care. His birth mom was homeless and couldn't take care of him.

She wasn't on drugs. They tested her for that. So, he's not one of those crack babies or anything. That's not why he's crying. Although, you know, his foster mom told me stories of people who said the nastiest things to her in public because her foster kids were acting out, but it wasn't even their fault because some of them had moms who WERE on drugs, so their behaviors really weren't their fault. It just goes to show you that we never know the whole story, huh?"

Stranger: "Oh. I would have never known he was adopted."

Me: "We are getting that a lot."

The reactions from strangers were varied, but usually tame. It was the questions from people we knew well that were surprisingly ignorant and often offensive. Let me just clear some things up with a little Q & A for the curious minded among you:

## Q: You're adopting. That's nice, I guess. Couldn't you have a real baby?

A: If (obviously there is no "if") you are asking if I have fertility problems, the answer is no—my lady parts are all fine and functioning, thanks for asking. We actually chose adoption of our own free will, because we are just better people than you, *I guess*. We could have had a "real" baby, but, really, who has time for all those OB-GYN appointments, co-pays, and sleepless nights? Adoption out of foster care is free and left my vagina 100% intact. So, no contest, right? Of course, if I *did* have fertility issues I'm sure your question still wouldn't have offended me in the least or sent me running toward the nearest bathroom stall for a good cry. Perhaps you should look up "The Wizard of Oz" on *Yelp* as you seem to be missing both a brain and a heart.

**Q: Aren't you worried that he won't love you as much as he loves his real mom?**

A: The fact that I blog and have previously chosen to publish a story about the time he needed a prostate exam because he wouldn't potty train could possibly lead to a little love lost when he is old enough to figure it out but, in reality, what he will be when he grows up is this: a guy. I don't know many grown men who sit around picking petals off of daisies chanting, "I love her, I love her not," especially about their mothers. Maybe I should be worried, but right now I AM THE REAL MOM of a six-year-old boy, so I have more urgent things to ponder, like how to get melted action figures off the front porch.

**Q: Are you worried about him being compared to your biological kids?**

A: Not really. He is our only boy, so he is unique by default. The only thing that really concerns me about mixing adopted kids and biological kids is them getting to be teenagers and knowing that they are not biologically related. It better not get all *Flowers in the Attic* up in here. That's all I'm going to say.

**Q: Would you do it again?**

A: Look, it is no walk in the park to take in a child who had a rough start in life. It hasn't been easy, and I do not intend to sugar coat it. Since his adoption, my son has been diagnosed with several special needs and we have spent a large chunk of time with therapists and specialists and in IEP meetings, but there is no guarantee that those things would not have happened with a biological child.

The truth is that the process of adopting and parenting our son has been a wild ride that I would not trade for the world. It revealed a strength that I did not know I possessed—the kind that only comes from God—which became the foundation for rebuilding a shattered faith, a shaky marriage and parenting not just one but three beautiful children. Yes, I would do it again.

## Q: Do you have any other advice?

A: Yes, for the love of God, when someone announces that a child has been/is going to be adopted, the ONLY response you should let escape your mouth is, "That's wonderful! Congratulations."

*Stephanie is a wife and mother of three who spends her days sticking out like a sore thumb in the middle of Amish country. More of Stephanie's writing can be found on her blog,* Binkies and Briefcases *and on* stephaniegiese.com. *She has been previously featured on* In The Powder Room *and* The Huffington Post. *Stephanie made her debut in print as one of the co-authors of the humor anthology* I Just Want to Pee Alone. *Her first children's book is scheduled for release in 2014. Connect with her on Twitter* @binkiesandbrief.

# Friends Let Friends Pee Their Pants

*by Rebecca Gallagher*

My friend Stacey and I had known each other since 2nd grade. We were pretty much attached at the hip.

By the time we were in high school, we had a secret language established. Well, it wasn't really secret. We thought we'd try Pig Latin but never achieved fluency. Basically our language was a silent exchange of facial expressions that succeeded in cracking each other up.

We loved Taco Bell, John Hughes movies and trips to the mall. What 14-year-old in 1986 didn't like those things?

On one particular cloudy summer day, I had been at her house hanging out. When you're in 9th grade, you don't play at your friend's house. You hang out. So we were hanging out. We probably spent the better part of the day in her room, listening to music— I'm guessing Duran Duran or Pet Shop Boys—reading *Seventeen* magazines, and talking about boys. Or talking about Mexican food. We both loved Mexican food.

Anyway, the day started off cool and cloudy so I had left my house in a pair of jeans. But by the time the clouds burned off that afternoon, it was pretty warm and I asked her if I could borrow a pair of shorts.

I remember she handed me a pair of cotton khaki shorts. They were cute and loose around the legs. We didn't share clothes much at all, despite our close friendship. Her mom was kind of against it. She didn't seem to want Stacey's clothes randomly left around other homes in the neighborhood. Whatever their hard-earned money bought for Stacey to wear wasn't to be traded back and forth. I could understand that. Our sizes were similar but our styles were different. Stacey was more boho chic, and I was more preppy collegiate. Well, to be honest, we were both dorks and wearing whatever sale clothes our moms found at Sears or Macy's.

Anyway, we had grown bored with our activities of just hanging out and her mom needed to make a trip to Kmart. We figured we would tag along. It was a way to get out of the house at least.

There aren't any Kmarts in my town these days. But if you remember the Kmarts of the '80s, they all had a photo booth at the front of the store.

After browsing the aisles and not finding anything that entertained or interested us, we decided to go in the photo booth and check it out. Her mom was busy enough with filling her cart from her shopping list, so we had time to kill.

One of us must have brought enough money for the photo booth. I don't remember exactly. I also don't remember where those pictures ended up; what I do remember was trying to pose for the camera—and what happened next.

There was a stool in the middle of the booth. We both tried to sit on it at the same time. But one of us kept sliding off. You could spin it around to make it higher or lower so you could set yourself up in the frame. For some reason, this action of trying to spin the stool to position it properly and falling off and cracking jokes, was hilarious. I mean, pee-your-pants-hilarious.

Literally.

I actually. Peed. My. Pants.

Oh dear GOD! What have I done? Then I started laughing so hard about the fact that I was laughing hard enough to pee my pants!

I tried to speak. You know when you're laughing so hard but no air comes out? When the words can't be heard and you just move your mouth? When tears are streaming down your face and your movement is somewhat hampered since there's actual air restriction to your brain? Yeah. That. I was having that moment. And then Stacey was laughing hard, but she wasn't laughing as hard as I was. Probably because she hadn't yet realized I had peed my pants. Well, HER pants.

So I worked on catching my breath. At this point there was a significant wet spot in the crotch region of the shorts. And I wheezed out, "I peed my pants."

Stacey, "What? No. You peed MY pants!"

Me, "I'm so sorry! Oh my gosh! I can't believe it! I'm so sorry!"

Of course, we were in the photo booth at the front of the store. So the attempt at whispering and stifling our laughter was probably unsuccessful. Who knows what the commotion sounded like to nearby shoppers.

I couldn't believe I had peed my pants. Her pants. This was so embarrassing. And in the middle of Kmart!

Stacey, "Maybe you should go use the restroom! Or did you relieve yourself enough in my pants?!"

Of course our sense of humor only added to the situation and we couldn't stop laughing. But I went to the restroom—the right way.

Nothing like wet urine in your shorts on a warm summer's day.

I was mortified at what her mom would think.

Me, "Please don't tell your mom!"

Stacey, "Well if she doesn't notice the wet spot, you'll be fine."

I knew her mom was a stickler with laundry. She did all the household's laundry and she was a fastidious housekeeper. I couldn't just put a pee-soaked pair of pants in Stacey's hamper and expect it to go undetected. Stacey would have some explaining to do!

Obviously hindsight tells me, who cares? I could've just told her mom I peed in the shorts because I was laughing too hard and I'm sorry for any added laundry it caused her. Surely after birthing two kids of her own, she could understand some slight urinary incontinence. Not that a 14-year-old typically suffers from incontinence, but laughter is quite powerful.

And so are the loyal bonds of friendship. We went back to Stacey's house. I rinsed the shorts in the bathroom sink and hung them over the towel rack in the bathroom. I changed back into my jeans, and I asked Stacey to tell her mom that I spilled soda on the shorts (whatever?) because at 14, I was still very self-conscious of the fact that I just peed my pants. Well, my friend's pants.

Now, as an adult woman who has birthed two watermelon heads down her vajayjay tunnel, I pee my own pants almost every day from the weakened bladder muscles. Trust me, I keep Poise pads in business. Whether it's from sneezing, laughing, Zumba class, or jumping on a trampoline, I have a low threshold of bladder control—sad, but true. But if my daughter had a friend who peed a pair of borrowed pants, I would assure her not to worry or be embarrassed. I would tell her the Kmart story so that we could laugh together.

Yes, I've been in photo booths since then. And I always use the restroom first.

*Rebecca Gallagher is a blogger, mom, wife and poop scooper, not necessarily in that order. She writes at her blog,* Frugalista Blog, *which isn't about couponing. She likes movies, Daniel Craig, tea and lip gloss. She can be found driving her mini van to PTA meetings and heading to Target in yoga pants and cashmere. She spends too much time on Pinterest checking beauty tips and not enough time cleaning her house. You can find her on Twitter @FrugieBlog.*

# Going Off the Deep End:
# A Tale of Swimsuits Gone Wrong

*by Andrea C.*

They say what doesn't kill you makes you stronger—and the stories of my bathing suits from summers past are no exception to the rule. If people have skeletons in their closet, mine are wearing swimwear—just hanging there as a reminder of the horrors I endured from poor choices, wrong sizes, and unsuitable designs for my body type. I will say that no matter how far I've come, when I hear the words *bathing suit*, the hairs (lots of them) on the back of my neck stand up straight, my stomach churns with anxiety, and my gag reflex is triggered. I'm here to tell you, however, that I'm finally over the trauma and the drama that accompanied these mistakes and if I can 'suit up' after everything that happened to me, then so can you.

As I look back to how my self-image in a bathing suit turned ugly, I have to, once again, climb up on the writing-for-therapy couch, put my head back and start remembering events from what I like to refer to as my Big Fat Greek Childhood.

It all started when I was ten and had reached puberty prematurely. My poor mom probably didn't even know how to react to her little girl having a Playboy-like figure in grade school, so when summer approached, she did what she thought was best. She made me an age-appropriate bathing suit that could accommodate my 32D cup without looking like Pamela Anderson on *Baywatch*. My mom was not a seamstress, but she knew her way around a sewing machine pretty well. She handed me a red bathing suit; it was a one-piece with a simple layer of ruffles at the top. Sounds like a lovely thing for her to make, right? Wrong. We had one BIG problem.

It was unlined.

It was a hot summer day and a bunch of girls from my grade were at the public pool hanging out and having fun swimming. A group of boy classmates made their way over to our side of the pool. They kept cheering me on to go off the diving board, making me think they were impressed with my diving skills. I finally realized, via one of my girlfriends, that it wasn't my diving skills they were gawking at—it was my see-through bathing suit that left absolutely nothing to the imagination. Apparently, I did look like Pamela Anderson in my bathing suit, only at least she had a liner. I quickly got dressed and called my mom to come and pick me up. That would go down in the history of my life as the most horrifying summer day ever.

Needless to say, she took me out to buy extra-heavy-duty, lined, Speedo-like, one-piece, competition-grade swim gear. Little did anyone know, it would be years—no, decades—before I'd ever be OK again in a bathing suit. I don't think I wore another bathing suit that entire summer. Money down the drain.

Then there was the element of hair. Being 100% Greek, I was already at an extreme disadvantage as far as excess-hair maintenance goes. At 12, 13, 14+ years old, what could we possibly know about a good, thorough, bathing-suit-ready type of shave? Nothing. Unless of course you remember the commercial for Nair with the roller-skating, short shorts-wearing girls. *We wear short shorts, but if you dare wear short shorts, Nair for short shorts.* So, after watching that commercial, a few of my Greek girlfriends and I got a brilliant idea to pool our money and buy some Nair to use before we went swimming. After slathering Nair all over our dark and hairy legs, we stared at each other in horror as it felt like we'd dipped them in hot lava. It burned and itched like nothing we could've imagined but we waited the elapsed time as directed on the bottle. After rinsing all of the hair away, we found that instead of thick black coarse hair we had bumpy red legs and inflamed skin from the chemical burns of the cream remover. We burned the shit out of that hair—and our beautiful, supple tween skin. Never again would Nair be the answer to hair removal for us. We later tried waxing (OUCH), the infamous Epilady torture device (HELL NO), and then resorted to good old-fashioned shaving with a razor and shaving cream. When it comes to bathing suits and being Greek, you're never fully shaven and if you are, you can expect a five o'clock shadow by noon.

Moving on to my college years, I took a course called *Dress for Success.* Let's face it, it was a filler course. Where some people took sports and what not—I was looking for an easy A to boost my GPA. The first day of class, the Professor announced we needed to wear a bathing suit under our clothes to the next class. I had already gained the "Freshman 15" plus more so this didn't sit well with me. But I did what I was told.

At the next class, she told us that we were going to get up on the very large fitting stand, one at a time, in our bathing suits, in front of everyone. Hands down at sides, legs slightly spread (still, no light was getting through my thighs), and—wait for it—she was going to take our picture to be used as a guide to help us understand our body shape, measurements, ratios—and basically pick apart what was wrong with us, in order to build it back up again in our favor. I should mention that, ironically enough, I wore a horizontal, wide-striped FUCHSIA and black one piece bathing suit. You don't have to guess that I was made an example of on the first day of this project.

"Andrea, can you get up here first and be our guinea pig?" (She lost me at "pig.")

She got her pointer out. (In hindsight, wow, did I exercise restraint in not grabbing that pointer and beating her with it . . .)

"Now here's a great example of why you should NEVER wear thick horizontal stripes. Andrea is 'busty' (as she aims pointer at my chest) and should *not* be wearing bright colors that draw attention to that area."

And she went on and on. For what seemed like half an hour, I was nothing but a DON'T—a big red circle with a slash through it for all to see. Luckily, my fellow college friends were also sporting the extra 15 or so pounds, so the combined looks of horror and sympathy on their faces really gave me a feeling of comfort while I was up there. The nice thing about going first was that I'd get it over with and be able to sit back and watch the other 20 girls go through being a *What Not to Wear* contestant before it was even a show.

As an adult, I realize that wearing a bathing suit or bikini is like parading around a beach in a bra and underwear that's made of a different material, right? Who feels comfortable doing that?

Maybe some—but the majority of us are all thinking the same things.

*Is my butt hanging out?*

*Are my boobs symmetrical when I lie down on my beach towel?*

*Did I miss a spot shaving?*

*Can you see my stretch marks?*

*C-section scar?*

*Fat rolls?*

*Cottage cheese?*

*Thigh dimples?*

Maybe I'm getting wiser in my old age but I say, who the hell cares? Men parade up and down the beach—hairy as monkeys, man boobs flopping in the summer breeze, and love handles galore. Most of the time—they don't care. They put their shit out there loud and proud. We need to learn a lesson from them and just say, screw it—this is who we are; and we are beautiful!

Now when I go to the beach, I put my hair in a stylish ponytail or wear a great looking hat, add a fabulous pair of earrings that make me feel pretty—followed by a sexy sarong and high-heeled sandals—and dammit I feel beautiful (despite the voices in my head telling me I should've stuck to my New Year's Resolutions.) Let's be honest, even if we had lost that ten pounds we'd hoped to, we'd still have a complaint about how we look in our bathing suits.

Go have fun at the beach—enjoy your time, your peace, your family—whatever. And give other women a smile when you see them walk by you at the beach—maybe even tell them you love their suit. What the hell—we're all in the same boat trying to feel good about ourselves.

Cheers and Happy Swimsuit Season (even if that *is* an oxymoron)!

*Andrea C., also known as "DG," is the one of the leading experts in the field of Domestic Engineering. She currently lives with her husband, three sons and three cats in the Lakes Region of New Hampshire where her days are filled with giggles, Legos, and an endless supply of Greek food. When she is not pretending to work, begrudgingly cleaning up urine from in and around the toilet, or dutifully cooking for an army, she gives her extra time to two local charities that provide clothing and personal hygiene supplies to underprivileged children. Andrea has been featured in* The Huffington Post *and was named one of* Circle of Moms' *Top 25 Funniest Mom Bloggers in 2012. Andrea is also a contributor to the best-selling book* I Just Want to Pee Alone. *Connect with DG on her blog,* Underachiever's Guide to Being a Domestic Goddess, *and on Twitter @DomesticGoddss.*

# Stranded on the Flood Plain
# of (Peri)Menopause:
# A Cautionary Tale

*by Deborah Quinn*

God, I hated my period when I was in high school. It seems to me one of Nature's cruelest jokes that just when my adolescent body was already subject to veritable tsunamis of emotion, ol' Aunt Flo would add monthly waves of *agita* that left me wracked and sobbing on my bed one or two days a month. Adding to my dismay were the cramps that sent me to the school nurse, muttering shame-facedly about "that time" and asking to lie down in her dim, antiseptic-smelling office. And let's not even mention that every month, like clockwork, one perfect zit would bloom on my chin, like a misplaced Rudolph nose, gleaming beyond the coverage capacity of any concealer ever invented.

The worst thing was that although I knew My Friend would show up somewhere in the midst of all this hormonal *Sturm und Drang*, I never knew exactly when. I'd be sitting in Earth Science, doodling the name of my latest crush in the margin of my notebook, then suddenly I'd be making a mad dash to the bathroom between classes, having to borrow a maxi-pad from the cool girls smoking in the last stall, and then waddling off to my next class. I didn't use a tampon until I was almost a senior in high school, for reasons I don't fully understand—maybe my mom didn't think it was "appropriate" or maybe I wasn't ready to negotiate the intricacies of my own plumbing until the ripe old age of 17.

Eventually those days passed—some combination of realizing that I was not, in fact, the center of the universe, and the birth control pills I started taking in college. Those pills stabilized everything. Aunt Flo came every month with no fuss or bother; a box of tampons could last for several months, and there were no surprises. And that's how it's been for the past few decades: despite the wear and tear caused by a preemie, a miscarriage, and a second child, my lady plumbing has run pretty smoothly.

Until now.

I went to my lady-parts doctor a year or so ago because I had gotten worried about the intensity of my periods: we're talking gushers, folks. We're talking entire boxes of super-plus-plus tampons being used up in three days. The doctor told me that no, in fact, I wasn't dying from some rare disease. She used a technical term to describe my condition: "You're just flooding," she said. "That's a sign of perimenopause."

Say *wha*? No one told me there was something that happened *before* menopause. I figured that I'd get through The Change with some hot flashes and dry skin, but would emerge on the other side with gleaming silver hair like Emmylou Harris and extra pocket money from never having to buy tampons again. I'd even thought about putting that tampon money in a jar and saving it up for a little me-splurge, the way people do when they're trying to quit smoking.

My friends, perimenopause is like Mother Nature's last joke. It's the swampy marshland of menopause: frequently flooded, difficult to map, and hard to recognize until you're in the middle of it. Here I am, teetering on the threshold of *omigod* 50, and my body is behaving as if I'm 16 once again: hormones carouse through my body like teenagers on a drunken joy ride, causing me to hate my children, my husband, my job, and pretty much anything else. I'd hate you too, without even knowing you, during Hormone Week. Yes, *week*. It's not a day or two any more. These hormones—perhaps because they've been relatively quiet for a few decades—they've developed *stamina*: they move in and start eating popcorn on the couch of my psyche.

I will say that at least I've got slightly better coping strategies now than I did when I was in high school—and no, it's not all about the fact that at my age I have legal access to the wine. I go for a walk, take a shower, go to sleep early, try to stay away from sharp knives lest I inadvertently threaten my husband with bodily injury for leaving his socks on the coffee table *again*.

Perimenopause means you're not yet a candidate for nicely regulated pharmaceutical hormones (which, probably, you don't really want anyway because of the whole maybe-they-give-you-cancer thing) so instead you're subject to periods as erratic as they were when you were 13.

And that's why I found myself the other day at my son's soccer practice doing that thing that parents do—half reading email, half watching the scrimmage—when suddenly . . . yep, there she was. Aunt Flo had shown up for soccer practice. There were 45 minutes of practice left, I was without tampons, and there was nowhere nearby that I could drive to for supplies and still make it back for the end of practice. The sidelines were mom-less; there were no cool girls smoking in the bathroom who might bail me out. In fact, there was barely a bathroom—just a slightly upscale porta-potty.

So. Yes. That was me the other day at soccer practice: a 50-year-old woman with a wad of toilet paper in her pants, hoping to avoid ruining yet another pair of underwear. It was a long practice and an even longer drive home.

Let my story be a lesson to you. Should you find yourself in this strange perimenopausal land, do not leave the house without a tampon stashed somewhere on your person. Tuck one behind your ear, if need be. And if you see a "Woman of a Certain Age" walking gingerly towards her car, don't be shy: slip her a tampon. She and her underwear will be incredibly grateful.

*Deborah Quinn is, variously, a writer, professor, wife, mother, and former PTA president of a Manhattan public school, an experience that has equipped her for a possible second career as a military diplomat. In 2011, after more than 20 years in NYC, she and her family moved to Abu Dhabi. Now she is ambivalent about two continents. Her work has been syndicated on* BlogHer *and she writes regularly for the Abu Dhabi newspaper,* The National. *She has written a YA novel titled* The Time Locket. *Connect with Deborah on her blog, MannahattaMamma.com, and on Twitter @MannahattaMamma.*

# Happy Accidents

*by Janel Mills*

Our third daughter was a surprise. Not an accident, exactly, because babies aren't things that you apologize for and forget about. Not a mistake, because who could ever regret a baby with bright orange hair and the chubbiest thighs in the history of chubby baby thighs? A surprise is something you didn't know was going to happen, something that catches you off-guard, something that might initially frighten or startle you, but quickly makes you feel happy and thankful.

Nobody wants to talk about surprise babies. Every married or committed couple with kids wants the world to believe that they are responsible, normal parents who planned out each and every one of their children. News flash: there's a whole lot of unprotected sex going on in this country, and it's not just happening on MTV between teenagers. Grown-ass women in their 30s and 40s are taking that week of Sex Ed. they had in 8th grade biology class and chucking it out the window on a regular basis in favor of wild, spontaneous sex. Maybe that's the *real* reason no one wants to admit that the youngest child with the eight-year gap between siblings was a surprise: because admitting *that* means admitting that one night, things got so hot between you two that you said, "FUCK IT, LET'S JUST *DO* THIS," laughing in the face of reproductive science.

However, when I tell a group of women that Surrey was our surprise baby, I usually get at least one knowing smile and nod. Then someone mentions which one of their kids was their surprise. Quite often it's the third. Three seems to be the magic number for a surprise baby. Probably because after having two kids, you're just thankful for any and all opportunities to have sex, and don't want to cloud your mind with dumb ideas like contraception.

My husband and I always said we wanted at least three kids. Maybe four, but definitely three. We would have three kids for sure and then discuss the possibility of a fourth. What we didn't discuss during those childless years when everything seemed so rational and logical and not covered with dried yogurt, was the possibility of having a child who could be so incredibly demanding, draining, and clingy that she made us stop to consider whether or not we could handle another child on top of caring for her and her sister. The problem, though, was that Rob did not possess the hormones that make a woman go temporarily insane and block out all of the logical reasons why she shouldn't have a baby. I, on the other hand, had more than enough for the both of us, and began my campaign for having another baby shortly after our second daughter's first birthday. We went back and forth for about six months—I would bombard my husband with crazy talk about a new baby, he would temporarily shut me down with boring shit like reality and facts. Then I would wait a month or so and bring it up all over again.

Finally, around Halloween, we struck a deal: all further talks of more babies would cease until our daughter's second birthday.

This would give my husband a good four months of blessed peace from the rantings of my baby fever-addled mind. I was happy with the compromise, and my baby fever actually passed. I decided that my husband was never going to budge and that I should just settle in and focus on raising the girls I already had.

So that's where I was mentally over two years ago. I genuinely didn't want to get pregnant, and I was starting to discover the perks of having two kids who weren't in baby territory anymore. Things were good. Babies could wait.

Then, shortly after Thanksgiving, I realized that even by the most fanciful mathematical calculations, my period was pretty goddamn late. Bought the test, did the wait, and boom—pregnant.

The first few weeks after finding out we were pregnant were so surreal. I kept apologizing to my husband, even though I had nothing to apologize for. I think part of me actually believed that I had willed myself pregnant through magical thinking. I wish that had been true, because if I had that power I was going to start using it for more useful things, like having burritos or briefcases full of money delivered to my house. I also felt guilty for not being as excited and happy as I should have been. All I could think about were the added costs a third child would bring with it, when I would be off work, whether my car would fit three car seats, and on and on. When I told one of my good friends, her first reaction was pure anxiety and the overwhelming need to buy a pregnancy test herself. She was a veteran of her own surprise pregnancy when I was pregnant with my second daughter, and was convinced that history was repeating itself. Guess what? *It was.* Which, honestly, didn't do much to dissuade me from my belief that I could mentally induce pregnancy through sheer brainpower.

Sometimes I shoot baby-thoughts from my brain at women I dislike. Oh, what's that, boss? You're going to have to write me up for being late to work? I think *you* better check the clock, and while you're at it, check a goddamn calendar, because YOU'RE THE ONE WHO'S LATE, BITCH.*

Toward the end of my first trimester, I realized a couple of things: first, after having two daughters, my husband and I had completely run out of girl names that we agreed on. Second, there's nothing like a surprise pregnancy to show you what your relationship is really made of. If you've spent the last few years building and repairing your marriage house with straw or twigs, you're going to be completely fucked when the big bad pregnancy test comes to blow your house down. Luckily, our house had been built, torn down, and then rebuilt again using sturdy bricks. Our surprise baby proved to us once and for all that we were a rock-solid team. Finally, I realized that people show up in your life when they're supposed to show up. That might not necessarily be convenient for you, but that's just how the universe works. Our sweet little ginger baby had an appointment to keep with us that following summer, and she wasn't going to be late.**

Just because someone shows up early to the party doesn't mean you're not still happy they came. But listen, everyone who's supposed to be here is now here, so I'm going to go ahead and lock the front door. If I hear anyone else knock on the door, I'm turning off the lights and hiding behind the goddamn couch.

---

*To be fair, my boss is a lovely woman, and I have never used my brain to shoot baby-waves at her. I am, however, late to work on a regular basis, and she should probably sit me down and have a serious conversation with me about that. But definitely not write me up, because that would not make her a lovely woman. It would probably end up making her a pregnant woman, if you know what I mean.

\*\*Actually, she was about a week late, but let's not ruin a nice moment here, shall we? Or did we already by adding this completely distracting footnote? Either way, I just wanted to make sure you knew that I survived a whole extra week of being unexpectedly pregnant in the middle of August in a house with NO AIR CONDITIONING. That's all. Proceed to the touching ending above.

*Janel Mills is a librarian raising three beautiful little girls with her beardedly gifted husband. Surprisingly, killer research skills and a knack for literary analysis have not helped her figure out how to get everyone dressed and out the door on time in the morning. She writes about raising a princess, a wild child, and the happiest toddler on Earth using as many curse words as possible on her blog* 649.133: Girls, the Care and Raising Of. *You can see how many times she can use the f-bomb within 140 characters on Twitter @649point133.*

# The Reason I Need a Chaperone

*by Kerry Rossow*

Lipstick on my teeth is the least of my worries. If I have lipstick on my teeth, it is still a win. "Yay, ME! I actually wore lipstick!"

I have a long history of, *ahem*, social mishaps.

So, I have surrounded myself with socially talented women—a support team, if you will. They know what is appropriate. They know when to shelve the f-bomb. They know when to keep their trap shut. They talk to me real slow and quiet-like so I understand that my actions have consequences.

Most importantly, they know when to rein me in. They recognize the signs and are aware of the social triggers that will send me into inappropriate hell.

I call them "Team Appropriate!"

The trouble is, they can't chaperone me 24 hours a day. I am often allowed in public on my own.

Had anyone on Team Appropriate been with me at the YMCA last year, they would have never let me get in that hot tub naked.

It was closing time and I found myself alone in the women's locker room, staring at the hot tub. As a mother of four, alone time is a rare and beautiful occasion. The hot tub was calling to me. How awesome would it be to sit in a hot tub? ALL ALONE? The only holdup was that I didn't have a swimsuit with me.

I told myself that it was almost closing time and no one else would be entering the locker room. *Probably not.*

Throwing caution to the wind, I enjoyed 22 seconds of heaven in the hot tub before I heard the creak of the door. I positioned myself to shield the intruder from my full frontal. Imagine my surprise when she stepped into the hot tub. Imagine Ms. Stepford-in-a-tankini's surprise when she got a look at Ms. October!

We both stared at the wall for answers.

She lasted in the hot tub for nine seconds.

She didn't even warn the young, hard body, swimmer type that she passed as she sprinted out of the locker room. What an inconsiderate bitch.

As Ms. Hard Body entered the hot tub, my embarrassment was replaced by irritation. *Can I not get a fucking minute to myself?* Instead of respectfully staring at the wall, Ms. Hard Body was staring at my 36WTF's like she was witnessing her parents having sex. Just as I was about to splash her, the locker room door creaked for a third time.

Why, hello! Come on in! Call your friends! Call your neighbors! It's a party! Step right up! It's a naked soccer mom!

The third witness to the naked show was a woman in a burka. That's right—the absolute epitome of modesty!

Had Team Appropriate been there, they would have told me to sit still, wait them out, cling to what was left of my dignity, and leave through the back door.

But no Team Appropriate in sight.

I panicked, and bolted. Ms. Modesty must have been horrified to see a naked woman leaping over a frightened Ms. Hard Body. Ms. Hard Body actually put her hands up in a defensive move. I'm still not sure if she wanted to shield her eyes (LOOK AWAY! LOOK AWAY!) or if she was afraid a loose boob was going to slap her face on the way by.

When I reported this incident to Team Appropriate, they all shook their heads and shared knowing glances. I should not be allowed out without a chaperone.

When I was planning to attend my first blogging conference, Team Appropriate became concerned that I would be travelling so far without support staff.

Team Appropriate decided they needed a pinch hitter. "Is there anyone that you know and trust attending the conference? Someone we can count on to guide you? Someone who isn't afraid to tackle you to the ground if you start to spiral out of control?"

"Why, yes, Team Appropriate! YES! I know just who to call!"

I immediately texted a fellow humor blogger, "You are in charge of keeping me from making an ass of myself at the conference!"

I should have realized that putting a humor blogger in charge of keeping me from making an ass of myself was like putting a fox in charge of the henhouse. But . . . I didn't.

With a plan in place and new shoes on my feet, I was ready!

A warning flag should have flown when my chaperone goosed me by way of an introduction on opening night. Without a flag in sight, I was having a blast. My chaperone and I yukked it up with some online pals, and I hit the open bar hard.

"Look at me! I'm at a conference! Look at me! I'm having uninterrupted conversations with adults! Look at me! I'm wearing clothes!"

Feeling all fancy and full of myself, I decided to step away from my support team. My chaperone was just a few feet away. I could see her. She could see me. If I got into trouble, I could just give her the panic eye and she would come to my rescue.

As I stepped away, I saw a small group of women fawning and drooling all over my favorite Home/DIY blogger. Clearly, I wasn't the only one who stalked her gorgeous blog. Clearly, I would wow her with my witty banter. Clearly, these other women were embarrassing themselves.

I casually stepped into the circle of worship. Wow, these women were small. I mean teeny. At almost 6 feet tall, I towered over them. They were like a herd of crazed Polly Pockets. A pause in conversation and all Polly Pocket eyes turned to me. The voice in my head said, "They are all staring at you, wondering who the Jolly Green Giant is. They are all on the fancy train and you are not invited."

But then, I met the eyes of my favorite blogger. She had the kindest eyes I had ever seen. She was so gracious when I introduced myself. But I could feel the train pulling away. I knew that my big moment was passing. The Polly Pockets wanted her back. Wanting to prolong our moment, I searched desperately for my witty banter. Out of nowhere, these words fell from my mouth, "Well, you are so cute and little. I could just breastfeed you!"

In slow motion, I saw the Polly Pocket next to me spit out her wine.

Where was Team Appropriate? My head was swimming and I could see my chaperone just a few feet away, bantering wit all over the damn place.

The train pulled out of the station.

Conference season is soon approaching and Team Appropriate is hard at work. A plan is in place. They have written several appropriate one-liners for me to memorize. If I find myself bedazzled and in the presence of my favorite writers, I vow to stick to the script. When I told Team Appropriate that my humor blogger/failed chaperone would be joining me for this year's conference, they suggested that maybe we should bring in someone with more experience. Someone with years of practice dealing with my social shortcomings and awkward outbursts.

So, I will be rocking the conference circuit this summer with my mother at my side! What a relief to know that I will have someone to cut my food, wipe my nose and remind me to stand up straight. The Polly Pockets are going to be so jealous.

*Kerry Rossow is a recovering teacher who decided to stay home, wrangle her four children and blog about her life shenanigans. Kerry tries to avoid restraining orders while she ~~stalks~~ features local houses on her blog,* HouseTalkN. *You can also find Kerry* In The Powder Room *sharing stories that make you feel better about yourself. Kerry joined some of the funniest mothers in the blogosphere to bring you the best selling book* I Just Want To Pee Alone. *Fulfilling a lifelong desire to perform on stage without throwing up, Kerry joined the cast of* Listen To Your Mother, Giving Mother's Day a Microphone. *You can keep up with Kerry's shenanigans on Twitter @HouseTalkN.*

# Is Forty Fabulous?

*by Ellen Williams and Erin Dymowski*

Across the country, fourth decade soirees play out weekend after weekend—women with perfect blowouts and killer heels celebrating the lives of their girlfriends by toasting their passage into middle age with style.

"Woot, woot! Happy Birthday, girl! Forty IS fabulous! We rock brilliant careers and can even start new ones while climbing mountains and running marathons!" Everyone shakes their feather boas, raises their hand-painted martini glasses and looks at all they have accomplished through their rose-colored novelty sunglasses. It's all so exhilarating!

But the party ends, the Spanx are shed and the feathers get packed away until the next "Forty is Fabulous" brouhaha. We are two friends, Ellen and Erin, who are both just over the crest of the big 4-0. This scene has played out for us over and over again. Until Beyoncé hits these digits and gives us a fresh anthem to jam to, Helen Reddy's "I Am Woman" will be our theme song. Hear us roar.

But we've been at this long enough and reflected over enough after-party chai tea to notice that little voice of skepticism whispering to our psyches that the glitz and glitter is a little cheap, the facade is a little askew. We've delved a bit deeper and pulled back the pretty wrappings to see what is *really* going on. And you know what we see? Bullshit.

A ton of deception is packaged in the "Forty is Fabulous" Trojan horse by camouflaging all of the pressures of the previous decades as some treasured gift. It fooled us for a little while, but we have seen the light. Or rather, we've met the evil bitch nemesis of "Forty is Fabulous," otherwise known as "Forty is The New Thirty."

If "Forty is Fabulous" was about celebrating being comfortable in your own skin, we would party on. If it was about liking the person you have grown into and loving the life you've chosen, we would fly that flag. But behind the high-fiving and booty-shaking is the God's honest truth: 40's fabulousness hinges on it posing as the previous decade.

Women are blitzed by the notion that we only deserve accolades if we don't actually look our age. None of our accomplishments seem to matter unless they are bundled with toned biceps and tight asses. Society has thrown down the gauntlet; but why, oh why, have we accepted the challenge?

It's enough to make both of us toss our wrinkle serums to the side, drop to our knees, and cry, "When does it end?" From the time of our first training bras, we have been bombarded with messages about what we should be and how we should look. We hoped that with time, society would just leave us alone. Looking at pictures of our mothers at our age with their easy-care short hair and their sensible shoes, they look frumpy by today's standards, but they also look happy, confident, and content. When did the expectations change? We know we are over the crest of the proverbial hill. It just feels like the descent is going to be rather graceless if we have to lug along and live up to the standards of our 30s: bikini bodies, glossy hair, and boundless energy.

Holy Oil of Olay, we just shellacked the past with a big heaping glop of "Glory Days." The reality is that we were both pregnant in our 30s, so "bikini bodies" is stretching it farther than even Lycra can endure; Erin didn't have the luxury of regular haircuts until last year when her youngest entered kindergarten; and we have both been tired for eons. We can either stay awake past 11 p.m. or wake up at 6 a.m., but not both in the same 12-hour cycle.

When our pores were smaller and our wrinkles were fainter, we were treading water in the Sea of Mothering Young Children, trying to save our identities while barely being able to hold our heads above water. Whether you're a stay-at-home mom or work for pay, the job of motherhood blankets everything.

Why, it was only just this year that we both were able to peek out from under that blanket of full-time parenting. After 15 years it was getting funky under there and it was high time to air out our truer, fuller selves. We are women who love writing, creating, and discussing ideas, so we started a blog. We threw our writing out there to be judged by the masses and to earn us money. Erin has returned to part-time teaching.

We are more content than ever before and we don't want to go back in time, and yet, we feel the pressure. For example, we work out for our health and we like to run, but why does that automatically mean "running a marathon" should top our bucket lists? In middle age are you somehow supposed to revert to childhood, where you need an award to prove, not just to yourself but to everybody else, how well you're getting on? Perhaps it's not really about the marathon per se, but the prestige of wearing the medal or slapping the 26.2 decal on your car to show you are better than the average middle-aged slug?

For the love of ibuprofen, Ellen already has arthritis behind her kneecaps and Erin has a bum ankle, so a marathon would be the height of lunacy, but what are we to fill our trophy shelves with to prove to the world that we are not aging without a fight? That's when a little thought slithers in, "I may not be able to run for miles, but a nice eye lift might put a spring in my step."

And that is where we have begun to feel uneasy. We may not feel THAT uncomfortable with how we look...but should we be trying to keep up? Should we care? Are we delusional to think that our packaging is adequate?

We have tried to put these insecurities to bed, but they can pop up by our sides again like toddlers hopped up on jelly beans, asking for one more bedtime story. Erin was recently mired in a conversation ranking procedures and treatments. You know, how injections "aren't really that big of a deal because it's not like you're going under the knife." Seems like a slope slippery with liposuctioned pudge to us.

A lip plumping injection is no tummy tuck for sure, but they are coming from the same place and that place doesn't look much different than a trophy shelf. They all broadcast the same thing: see how well I'm doing! See how youthful and energetic I am! See how you can't believe I have a teenager! Why don't women in their 40s have the bravery to shout from the rooftops, "I am happy, I am successful, and I deserve it because it has taken me forty years to get here!" Why can't they ignore the messages that tell them to fight aging with every tendon, dollar, and brain cell they have?

Here is our theory: the new midlife crisis is proving to the world you are not ACTUALLY having a midlife crisis. The classic crisis clichés, booze and Xanax, have been veiled with fitness and health so that women can still feel sanctimonious all the way to the doctor's office for that nip and tuck when they can't live up to expectations.

Blasted Botox! With all of this "betterment," what has actually been created is a constricting illusion of success: imaginary boxes to check off and molehills to climb. If women truly feel like they have made it, why can't they just kick back, sip a beverage, and enjoy the view? We're all for following dreams and pursuing goals, but when too many people share the same one—it makes us skeptical, especially when that goal is perfection. Exactly whose vapor trail are we all chasing?

Well here is our "Eureka" moment: this notion that "Forty is Fabulous" will only be genuine when we realize the things that make 40 a wonderful place to be AREN'T rock hard abs, perfect skin, or medals around our necks. What IS fabulous when you are 40 is enjoying your family and friendships that have taken you a lifetime to create. It's reveling in your skills after you have spent years tending to them and honing them. It's that sense of being comfortable in your own skin . . . even if it's sagging. It's embracing the fact that to be here, you have to let go of your younger self.

We want to live a life that's not posing as any other age or stage or time. We want to stand solidly in the here and now. We want to promote, embrace, and believe that the best thing you can aim for when you are 40 is being content with who you are. So let's kick that bitch "Forty is The New Thirty" to the curb. Now THAT is fabulous.

*Ellen Williams and Erin Dymowski are the dynamic writing duo sharing the blog,* The Sisterhood of the Sensible Moms, *but they don't share everything. Erin has 5 kids with her husband Steve* and Ellen has two kids with her husband Frank. They've got parenting covered from kindergarten to high school. Their blog is like a good Girls' Night Out conversation: full of shared stories, advice, book recommendations, and recipes; dosed heavily with humor and a dash of snark; and sprinkled with truth and honesty softened with sweetness. They are Pinterest ninjas, carpoolers extraordinaire, and Nikon warriors. They are pleased to be honored as BlogHer 2013 Humor Voices of the Year, but be sure to ask them about their gold medals in competitive synchronized litter box scooping, too. You can connect with them on Facebook, Pinterest, and Twitter @SensibleMoms.

# Skin Tag, You're It!

*by Julie Stamper*

When I was a teen, I worried about what people (especially my friends) thought of me. What if my hair isn't sprayed one foot off of my head? What if I don't like that new Simple Minds song? What if my outfit, like, gags them with a spoon? Not knowing how to operate a friendship yet, I didn't know if those relationships were very reliable and I trod carefully. Somehow, over the past 30 years, I've managed to maintain and strengthen those bonds with a group of six women who have known me since before I ever PMS'd.

Being friends with these women has been much like having kids. At the start, you're unsure of what to do, or who they will turn out to be. You're a little awkward; they're a little awkward. You both make mistakes. You hold their hair when they are throwing up and you hold their hand when they are sad. You kiss their boo-boos. You get angry when a boyfriend treats them badly. You get mad at their bad choices. You call them on their BS, and then you forgive. You cry at their weddings, and then you cry at their breakups and bad luck. You listen. You try to make it all better. In return you get hugs and love in spades. And you think they are the most beautiful, talented, smartest people you've ever known, and by some miracle, they think the same of you.

As we started to get married and have babies, and could easily have lost touch with each other, our group decided to get together every few years and have a mini-reunion. While these getaways began as a nice escape from diapers and vomit, they evolved over the years to become a safe place to be real and get down with our bad selves. Want to trot around in a swimsuit and not care if your flabby gut or varicose veins hang out? Work it! Want to overeat and get mildly drunk? I won't post the pictures! Need to fart? LOUDER!

So it's not unusual when things get a little up gross and personal between us. Like dealing with skin tags.

SCENE: It's a gorgeous Saturday afternoon in Scottsdale, Arizona. Our girlfriend reunion is on day three, and we've just left the spa. We're relaxed. We're happy. We're loosey goosey, baby, and we're hungry, so we pop in the deli next door. Divorced Friend is fresh off of flirting with her Russian masseur and is now flirting with the Italian guy working the deli counter and talking fresh mozzarella.

This gives OB-GYN Friend a moment to look me over.

OB-GYN KENOBI: Jude, you have a skin tag on your neck.

ME: I know.

OB-GYN KENOBI: I can take that off, you know.

ME: (*noncommittal*) Oh, great.

OB-GYN KENOBI: (*reaching toward my neck*) Here . . .

ME: (*jumping back in alarm*) What the hell? Do you mean right now?

OB-GYN KENOBI: (*hand twitching like Clint Eastwood's in* A Fistful of Dollars) Yes!

ME: Uh, NO, it will hurt, and this is a deli. Aren't there health laws in place?

FLIRTY FRIEND: (*Done flirting, turns around while waiting for sandwich*) What are you doing?

OB-GYN KENOBI: Pulling off Jude's skin tag. See it?

FLIRTY FRIEND: Let me see. (*She leans forward, reaches her hand up to look at it, and tears it from my body with her fingernails.*) OOH! OOH! I GOT IT! (*Raises her fingers in victory, holding a small piece of my DNA.*)

ME: AAAHHHH!

And then I make the major mistake, which I frequently do, of giving away too much information.

ME: I have a skin tag that is MUCH bigger than that one.

OB-GYN KENOBI: (*Gets crazy glint in her eye*) Where?

ME: (*Lifting my shirt to show my hip*) Right here.

GROUP: (*GASP!*)

This is no mere skin tag. It has actually progressed to the point where it looks like an Oompa Loompa, or a small toe that never developed fully. I have feelings for it. It's a part of me now. OB-GYN Kenobi's fingers start twitching again, and when we return to our rental house, she starts looking through drawers.

OB-GYN KENOBI: I'll need some scissors or dental floss and a topical anesthetic, stat. (*People start moving with purpose.*)

ME: No, that won't be necessary, because my little bud isn't coming off today.

OB-GYN KENOBI: It will only take a second, and it won't hurt.

ME: Yes, it will. I have to have a few drinks before this goes down.

OB-GYN KENOBI: Okay, but it's coming off.

I feed OB-GYN Kenobi margaritas in hopes she'll forget about my skin tag. She doesn't, and soon she is tying off my nubbin with dental floss. I'm frozen and whimpering, terrified. She stands up, brushes off her hands, and says in a deeply satisfied voice, "There. It will be dead soon. And then I am going to cut it off at the base."

I look down at my hip, and there is the most ridiculous looking dental floss bow, tied around my now incredibly revolting skin tag. It's so funny that I start to laugh, which makes me pee, so I flee to the bathroom. There I am, semi-wetting my pants in my swimsuit bottom with a huge dental floss bow around my skin tag. It is too much. I resolve that if the skin tag must go, I must be the one to cut it. It's mine. And Dr. Margarita Scissorhands isn't getting near it.

I pull the nail clippers out of my makeup bag, and tell my Oompa Loompa goodbye. I position the clippers, turn my head, and clip it off. MOTHER F! It hurts! And it's bleeding! What do I do with it? Should it have a proper burial? I wrap it in tissue, throw it in the garbage and walk back outside, proudly showing off my Do-It-Yourself surgery. All applaud my bravery.

ME: I did it! I took it off!

OB-GYN KENOBI: I'm very proud of you. But I would've gotten it at the base.

PERKY TITTIES FRIEND (*who is quite attractive*): I have a skin tag!

OB-GYN KENOBI: Let me see. (*She looks, and dismisses.*) No, yours are cute on you.

Uh, what? Skin tags on me are so revolting that they must be torn mercilessly from my body in a deli, strapped down with floss, and clipped immediately, but on Perky Titties with her size 0 jeans, they are *attractive*?! I resolve to take my clipped skin tag out of the garbage and Gorilla Glue it to Perky Titties' hip in the night.

Some people never have a true friend in their lives, but lucky me! I have six! It's like I won the friendship lottery! Except that it isn't like that at all. It's more like being married, or having children. It's hard work to keep up with each other's lives across states and in the middle of your own crazy existence, but when you stick it out and put your heart into it, it turns into this lifetime commitment of knowing when someone truly has your back.

Or at least will take your skin tags off of it.

*Julie Stamper is a mother of three teen-ish people and is a Master Columnist. She blogs at ADayInTheWife.com, where she documents the mastery of ruining childhoods and being dirty, both literally and figuratively. She's on Twitter at @JulieTheWife and Facebook at A Day In The Wife, but has only started to dabble in the crack that is Pinterest.*

# "Good Vibrations"?
# There's an App for That. Of Course There Is

*by Dawn Weber*

It has, um, come to my attention that the list of things your smartphone can do includes . . .

. . . *you.*

That's right. And just when you thought it was safe to borrow someone else's cell phone, you should now run—terrified and screaming—away from that idea until you find the nearest vat of bleach.

Perhaps I should explain. There I was the other day, bored, minding my own—you know, just living out my life of quiet desperation, when I decided I should get some meaningful work done.

So I pulled up Google's Android market, Google Play, to download a few useful, productive apps, such as "Bike Race" and "Subway Surfer."

That's when I found this: "Sexy Vibes."

And then I ran—terrified and screaming—in search of that vat of bleach.

Yes, it appears people download "Sexy Vibes," turn it on (so to speak), and commence rubbing their actual cell phones on their actual personal regions.

Truly, the end of days is nigh.

Mobile phones have always had a "vibrate" mode for calls; but thanks to the creators of apps like "Sexy Vibes," the function can be switched on for as long as needed, or until a "goal" is achieved.

Folks are now using cell phones to baste their turkey, to abuse their fuse. They're patting the bunny, double-clicking the mouse, five-finger shuffling, getting a little me-time—with their phones.

Let me repeat that so it sinks in: PEOPLE ARE MASTURBATING WITH THEIR PHONES.

Things of this nature are enough to send an OCD germaphobe like me—terrified and screaming—over the edge. Please tell me: what causes a reasonably sane person to look at a phone in such an, um, amorous manner? Jim Morrison was wrong; people aren't strange. People are fucking weird. And they're getting weirder all the time.

I will admit that I can see one advantage to a cell phone vibrator app: the recharge-ability factor. I may or may not have a "friend" who, um, may or may not possess an entire drawer full of marital aids, all of which she may or may not be able to use because the batteries are dead.

And these aren't just any batteries, she tells me, these aren't just AAs; these are the itty-bitty, son-of-a-bitch specialized electronic batteries, the ones that all look the same but have numbers like "CR209-OMGFU-7." She always forgets to remove the batteries and put them in my, er, *her* purse, in order to find replacements at the store.

That's what she tells me, anyway.

I figured the rest of my posse would be similarly amused/disgusted by "Sexy Vibes," and I was right. As always, the ladies did not let me down.

My friends' reactions ran the gamut from customer-driven:

"Talk about great phone service!" said Mari.

To declarations of devotion:

"I've often said I love my smartphone more than I should love a thing," said Beth, "but I didn't know it could love me back."

To jealousy amongst gadgets:

"Great," said Gaynell, "now my shower massager will be jealous of my cell phone."

To location, location, location:

"Now I know why some women keep their phones in their front pocket," mused Robin.

To smartphone shunning:

"I will never ask to see someone's cell phone again," said Sarah.

Me neither, Sarah, me neither.

I did a little more online research—that is just the kind of investigative journalist I am—and I found more than 110 other vibrator programs on Google Play, most costing around 99 cents: "Smart Vibrator," "Fun Vibrator," "Magic Vibrator," "Vibrator Dildo." There are also the plain vanilla vibe apps: "Vibrator: Classic," the very promising "Epic Vibrator," and the aptly named, "Zing Zing Wing Wing (Vibrator)." And, iPhone users rejoice, for you also have several choices, including "iBrateVibrate," "iVibe Massager" and the plain but capable-sounding "Sex Toy."

As with all apps, Google Play members can leave feedback on these utilities. Dozens of user/geniuses have written a variety of badly misspelled, moronic observations. Commenters ranged from jealous boyfriends:

"My girlfriend likes my Android phone more than me! I feel so jealous of my Android! Dammit!"

To, *ahem*, gushing devotees:

"Im in lov, daam! Absolutely fabulace! God I feel so alive! Who needs men!" (sic)

To the hygienically concerned:

"Wow. I love it. I put it in a little baggie!"

To future traffic fatalities:

"I use it all the time when I'm driving! All u have to do is slide up and down on ur phone." (sic)

To West Virginians:

"This app sucks. waste of time, I accidentally penis-dialed my granny." (sic)

*Sigh.* You know, I try not to judge; I am not a prude. I mean, who hasn't snuck a peek at porn? Who hasn't considered the possibilities of the vibrating chair?

Who among us doesn't have a drawer full of sex toys with dead, itty-bitty, son-of-a-bitch batteries?

Oh. That's just me?

And I had already heard about items such as the "Boditalk," a vibrator, and this is key—it's a SEPARATE vibrator—that is wirelessly activated by mobile phone conversations.

But for all my garden-variety knowledge and perviness and drawer full of dead "personal massagers," I have never, ever glanced at a Motorola with a gleam in my eye. Anyway, I don't know about you, but I lose my phone enough—I don't need to misplace it in the metaphorical deep end.

OK—I'm done. I'll get off my dirty digital soapbox.

But in the meantime, I'm here to help all the geniuses over at Google Play: I can save each of you randy bastards 99 cents, because you don't require any of these apps. Tell me, Einsteins: are you lonely? Bereft? Just flat-out horny? Do you miss your spouse, your partner, your lover? You don't need "Sexy Vibes," "Vibrator: Classic," or "Epic Vibrator." You don't even need "Zing Zing Wing Wing (Vibrator)." Just have someone—preferably not your grandmother (unless you're a West Virginian)—call you...in vibrate mode, repeatedly, or until your, um, "goal" is achieved.

Well, I sure am happy to bring you this hard-hitting journalism. I think we've all learned something, and here it is: on this planet, there is no end to the many and various things that people will attempt to hump.

And some folks really love their phones.

In the Biblical sense.

Apparently.

*Dawn Weber is a wife of one (she thinks) a mother of two (that she knows of) a blogger at LightenUpWeber.blogspot.com and the writer of the "Lighten Up!" newspaper column in the Buckeye Lake Beacon, for which she won the 2011 National Society of Newspaper Columnists third place, humor award. She currently resides in Brownsville, Ohio (Motto: Indoor Plumbing Optional) with her family and an ever-changing series of dirty, ill-mannered pets. Her goals include thinner thighs, a nap, maybe a solo trip to Walmart. Connect with Dawn on Twitter @DawnLightenUp.*

# My Life as a Moo Cow

*by Robyn Welling*

I don't like to think about breastfeeding.

It isn't because the subject makes me uncomfortable. Nor is it because I hate controversy, even though people seem to get more riled up about other women's breast/bottle decisions than over whether or not schools should teach that God was carrying a handgun when he invented global warming as a punishment for Bert and Ernie being homosexual for dinosaurs. And it certainly isn't because I'm against it—on the contrary. No, I don't like to think about breastfeeding simply because it leads to math.

I'm not a huge fan of math under the best circumstances, but now that I'm nursing my third kid I can't help but find myself tallying up Time Served in my head on a semi-daily basis. Those equations are the worst.

*If Breasts A and B travel at 155 mph toward the nursery at 3 a.m. to answer the call of a screaming infant who was just fed ten minutes ago, and are subsequently suckled upon nonstop for 15 months, and two years later Breasts D and F, already dragging on the ground, get manhandled for another 12 months, and after a six-year hiatus Breasts Y and Pffffth manage to re-inflate themselves for the dubious honor of another round of cracked nipples and midnight engorgement, how long will it be before Mommy loses her ever-loving mind and just wants her boobs back?*

Don't get me wrong—I love breastfeeding. On top of that, I barely use the dang things for anything else, so it's not like I'm missing out on a lucrative stripping career during this period of my life when, at any given moment, old Funbag and Flapjack might differ by several cup sizes based on where we are in the feeding cycle. But while I'm holding my darling baby curled against my chest, the soft amber glow of evening light sifting gently through the window as I silently pray for her to *just fall asleep already*, part of my brain is adding up months, calculating her age, realizing that I've spent over four years of my life catering to the orally-fixated whims of my offspring.

Four years? That's a long time to share custody of your own body.

And before you start doing some math of your own (four years, divided by three kids, multiplied by . . . WTF?), the answer is yes, I've forgotten how to wean. My first two babies just sort of . . . stopped. My third baby appears to be perfectly content with me continuing to provide her with beverages indefinitely, or at least until she realizes that she won't be able to cram my boobs in a cooler and sneak them into an underage drinking party when she's 17. Breast milk makes a terrible mixer with tequila, anyway.

I suppose that's no big deal, considering I'm not personally in any kind of a huge hurry for her to stop—it's not like I have it so rough. Sure, people look at me funny when she gets cranky and I have a 34-pound toddler plaintively requesting access to her fleshy pacifiers in line at the supermarket, but I don't care about that. Plus, as a work-at-home mom, I'm not faced with the challenges of pumping in an office, like I was with my previous kids. Not only was the electric breast pump heavy and cumbersome with its tubes and Madonna-inspired boob cones and unnatural suction, but one time even the presumed safety of a locked door was stripped from me when a construction worker, unaware of my presence, removed the door from its hinges and was confronted with a half-naked screaming woman who appeared to be under attack from a hyperventilating mechanical octopus.

No, the main problem with nursing my daughter isn't that it's a burden or an embarrassment; it's just getting impractical. As she hits stride in her terrible twos, Mommy occasionally needs a little liquid assistance. Unfortunately, it's been increasingly difficult to properly coordinate my caffeine and wine consumption so that it doesn't interfere with our topless time together. Also, I write while she nurses and naps, which means only one arm can be used for typing—a laboriously slow hunt-and-peck, just because she's feeling peckish. Meanwhile, I have older children wandering around the house, likely wishing their mom's upper deck wasn't on constant display like the à la carte counter in a 24-hour open-air café. Oh, and then there's the overzealous hooter honking. Out in public is bad enough, but pretty soon the absent-minded grabbing and tugging while she's sipping at the tap is going to be enough to bust the old bonbons. Note to baby: those aren't twist-off caps.

I often hear the voices of the Helpers, the older women who tell me to "Enjoy them while they're young." Sometimes, in the throes of sleep deprivation and general all-purpose annoyance, I have a momentary desire to roundhouse kick the Helpers directly in the blue hair. I marvel that these self-proclaimed experts don't understand the allure of breaking the invisible leash, the one that tethers my child's increasingly toothy mouth to my cowering nips and makes her feel entitled to lift my shirt wherever she feels like it, including Target's housewares department or at large family gatherings with my in-laws.

But deep down, I know they're right. I've been there before. I know I'll miss the precious bonding time we have together. I know I'll miss my threadbare nipples being her Velveteen Rabbit, and I know that, despite the damage, one day they'll be reborn as new, if somewhat sunken, well-loved sweater bunnies.

So I struggle to let her break the skin-binkie habit at her own pace. While doing my usual mental math, adding up the months and years when my breasts have not been entirely my own, I try to remember that the days are counting down in the other direction, too. In the near future, there will be a time when she no longer needs the comfort of my cantaloupes-turned-croutons. It will surely tug at my heartstrings when I realize that the last time I nursed my baby slipped by without fanfare, and all those moments we spent quietly embracing, mother and child, the tenderness of which will stay with me for the rest of my days, won't even be counted among her earliest memories. Eventually she'll be weaned and I'll have my body back, yet I have no doubt it will be a bittersweet victory.

But please don't let my cartwheels and champagne fool you into thinking otherwise.


*Robyn Welling is a freelance writer and humorist at* Hollow Tree Ventures, *where she isn't afraid to embarrass herself—and frequently does. She loves sarcasm, sleep, beer, other bottled items, long walks on the beach, and her husband. Oh, and her kids are OK, too. Her goals include becoming independently wealthy, followed by world domination and getting her children to clean their rooms. Until then, she'll just fold laundry and write about the shortcuts she takes on her journey to becoming a somewhat passable wife, mother, and human being. If history is any guide, she'll miss the mark entirely; join her as she bumbles her way through life on Twitter @RobynHTV.*

# Fugitives

*by Liz Dawes*

I watch her as she wakes. She stirs, turns over, and rubs her eyes as her lids flicker, open and shut, open and shut. She hates to wake up.

She sits, slowly, bleary and crumpled and grumpy. Her face is pale, grey shadows printed beneath her eyes, and white, translucent skin. She wears the day heavily, even now. As though it has defeated her before it begins. At seven-years-old, she is too young to be this weary.

One of the things you learn about autism is just how tiring it can be. She works twice as hard as other kids. That's not a throw away turn of phrase, but a simple statement of fact. We all learn an academic curriculum, and for most kids that's hard enough. But she has double the work of a typical child. That which comes naturally to others is not hard-wired in her, nor will it ever be. She is bright, so she will learn, but learn she must. With each numeracy and literacy task comes a lesson from the social curriculum. A private lesson, with no rules, no facts, and no one to teach her. She makes her way through the social parts of her day by trial and error; and children can be cruel when she gets it wrong. It's no wonder she's exhausted.

"I don't *want* to go to school Mamma!" She is petulant now. Childish anger rising at the injustice of the burden she is asked to bear. I am stern. It is a school day, she is not ill, and she must therefore attend. Those are the rules, I tell her. And for the first time in a while she does not fight me. She just cries. Big fat tears roll down her blotchy cheeks. Pink rosebud lips wobble. Her head flops forwards and her shoulders droop. Her voice is barely even a whisper: "Mamma! Please Mamma!" She is shattered. She falls back on her pillow, gazing at the middle distance. Defeated.

She is my other half. Her blonde to my brunette. Her blue eyes to my brown. Like a negative to a photograph, there is no me without her. She is youthful and impatient and headstrong, but today she has no courage left, and I can see no point in pushing her further. I pick up her hand.

"We have to take your brother to school, my love. You need to get up. But listen, just this once—*just this once*—we will hide you under a blanket in the car and tell the teachers you are ill. And you can spend the day with me. OK?"

She props herself onto her elbow, and rubs at the tears with her favourite bear. "But . . . " and with a frown, "I am not ill, Mamma."

"I know darling. But I have to give the school a very good reason for you not attending today and being a bit tired isn't going to be good enough. So I will tell them that you are ill. Otherwise they will make me take you to school."

"You mean . . . " a pause, and then, "we are going to lie to the teachers?"

That's exactly what we are going to do. And this is the trouble. I want to give her a break. I want to accommodate her struggles, because she *is* exhausted. But now my conscience is reminding me of bad examples, and slippery slopes and consistent parenting, and honesty being the best policy but I look at her grey little face and I can't. I just can't. A deep breath.

"Yes. We are going to lie. It's that or I have to take you to school, and I don't think you'll manage school today."

I watch as she processes the information. Rather than just grab the opportunity, she considers its implications. "Will you get arrested?"

I hide a smile. I'm rather proud of her for caring about me instead of taking the easy way out. "No, my love. It's not a crime to lie to teachers. It's not something we should do very often, but it's not a crime."

She's sitting upright now, considering the plan. Interested. "But we might have to spend the day hiding out and sneaking around in case we get caught! Just in case? I think our headmistress has spies . . . we should run away to Timbuktu!" A twinkle in her eyes now, a spark of life. Her cheeks are beginning to look pink again. "Some people think that's the capital of Mali Mamma but it isn't. It's just a very important city. To them." I breathe out. That's my girl. My little professor. My walking book of facts. I play along with the game as it forms in her head.

"That's very true. We'll have to be really, really careful. But I think we might just make it."

She jumps out of bed. "Let's do it, Mamma!"

Plans are made, strategies worked out. She chats non-stop, organising me and her brother; him in simple commands, me in comic asides. "I am very poorly today," she announces in her best stage voice to him. Then in dramatic whispers: "*Let's not tell him so he won't accidentally tell the teachers!"* She knows him well. He'd rat us out for a bar of chocolate without a second thought.

She tells me that, after he is safely at school, we will play her favourite game. I will drive, and she will sit next to me, telling me exactly where to go. She is in charge, planning and dodging a clever route through the back streets of London as we evade justice and make good our escape. Wherever she commands, I will go. We will discover new towns, new landmarks, new hideouts. And we will almost definitely find cake and hot chocolate too. What fugitive could want more?

As we arrive at the school car park she collapses into a half-conscious doze, eyelids drooping, hand clutching forehead. I could swear she almost breaks into a fever. They say autistic children are observant mimics. Mine gives a master class in acting this morning. She stays in the car, I drop her brother, and we're off.

As we leave she sits up, shakes her head, and regains her normal health. We reach the gates, and she becomes my navigator, head cocked to one side in thought, arms hovering, ready to point. And then a decision: "Turn left Mamma!" and the adventure begins. But as we leave the gates we drive past a teacher, who sees her, head thrown back, eyes twinkling, her whole body laughing as we make our getaway. We are rumbled.

But we don't care. We are fugitives, she and I. Thelma and Louise. Butch and Sundance. Riding through town in our metal steed, dodging the cops and getting lost in the alleyways. Secretive and sneaky and halfway to Timbuktu.

*Liz Dawes is a creative writer, editor, and copywriter, and a staff writer at* In The Powder Room. *She is also a weekly columnist for* Fighting Fifty, *and is finishing her first book. When not writing, Liz is a mother, gardener and lover of gin o'clock. She lives between London and the South coast of England with her two children, husband, stepdaughter and collection of ungrateful and willfully disobedient pets. Liz can be found over at her writing business, LiveLifeWrite.com, and on Twitter @LizDawes.*

# What Happens in Vegas

*by Shari Simpson*

Picture, if you will, three women with Brazilian-straightened hair, sparkly bustiers, Spanx-free racehorse thighs and bounce-a-quarter-off-'em abs. They are playing slot machines with one hand, guzzling guava-tinis with the other, fending off the advances of muscled, mustachioed men named Clint with a well-placed elbow, and laughing in shrill, devil-may-care, what-happens-in-Vegas-you-know-the-rest voices.

Now completely forget all of that.

*Vegas.*

Sure, it's a city in Nevada, but it's also a state of mind.

Every Thursday morning at 9:30 a.m. for the past eight years, (416 Thursday mornings, if you do the math), I've been meeting with my best friends, Pickles and Aunt Candy, for a group we call *Vegas.* Oh, aren't you smart. Yes, Pickles and Aunt Candy are not their real names. Nobody uses their real names in *Vegas.* And as we all know, what happens in *Vegas,* stays in *Vegas.*

But here's ten cents for the peepshow for you.

We meet for talk. We meet for miracles. We meet for a haven. We meet for support. We meet for truth telling. We meet for prayer. We meet for sanity. We meet for sobbing. We meet for laughter. We meet for hope.

Oh, and coffee. We meet for coffee.

### Talk

According to a recent study published in the *Journal of Neuroscience*, women have 30% more "language protein" in their brains than men. Let's just say the researchers could have saved themselves a lot of money and lab time by hanging out in *Vegas*. And the coffee is better.

### Miracles

There have been many, but I will single out The Miracle of The Underpants.

A few years ago, during a particularly stressful financial period, when my husband and I were literally collecting pennies to pay for milk, I looked at my ancient, raggedy underpants in despair and prayed, "God, I know there are people in true poverty, so I'm fairly embarrassed to pray this to you, but you say you meet all our needs without judgment. So, God, *I need underpants.* I don't *want* underpants, I *need* underpants. Because mine are falling down around my thighs, which completely undermines the purpose of underpants. But you already know that. Uh . . . Amen?"

The next day at *Vegas*, Aunt Candy walked in the door and said with some hesitation, "I hope this doesn't sound too skeevy, but I bought these underpants and they're the wrong size. I swear I only know that from the package, not from trying them on. I don't suppose you'd want them?"

Ladies and Gentlemen, The Miracle of The Underpants.

### *A Haven*

As you can imagine, there have been many changes over the past eight years. One of us had a baby. One of us had a painful divorce. One of us went into marriage counseling. All of us, at one time or another, have said to each other, "I'd rather be married to you."

### *Support*

For two of the eight years of *Vegas*, I was awash in a sea of tiny papers. My son was obsessed with the alphabet, and I mean *obsessed,* as in the lowercase letters were considering a restraining order against him. Thus, I spent every day, for two solid years, cutting out the alphabet. Every. Day. Free hand. With poultry shears. From construction paper, printer paper, newspaper, paper towels, and toilet paper. And the letters had to be cut out new every day, because as all grocers and three-year-old boys know, letters don't stay fresh overnight. Thank you, sweet Jesus, for Thursday's letters, because 26 divided by Mommy, Aunt Candy and Pickles equals a much happier number.

### *Truth Telling*

There is a special sort of friendship that is born through hard truth. Like when *Vegas* has to tell you that your house smells like pee. Granted, this was not exactly shocking news, as I had two children under the age of two and a couple of maliciously incontinent pugs, but still. When *Vegas* summons the courage to tell you that your entire domain reeks of piss, you have to appreciate that honesty. And, of course, great truth can lead to true revelation. A few weeks later I was able to share with *Vegas* my deeper understanding of the pee semi-mystery, because I had caught my daughter lifting the little removable pot out of her Dora training potty and drinking her own urine. With some splash factor. (This story, of course, did not stay in *Vegas*, but was told so often and so widely that it has taken on the mystique of an urban myth.)

### *Prayer*

This could be subtitled "sanity," "sobbing," "laughter," and certainly, truly, fundamentally, "hope." *Vegas* does not exist because we are three women looking to each other for answers. We are looking up. Encouraging each other, loving each other, guffawing at each other, telling the truth to each other, and holding each other when it just hurts too much for words, but looking up for that which we cannot give each other. Together.

This morning, *Vegas* took place for ten minutes in Aunt Candy's sassy red rented car. She was leaving town, Pickles had to get to work, and I had to be done quickly because my husband was home and had scheduled sex for 10 a.m. I carried three cups of coffee out to the car and the conversation proceeded as follows:

> AUNT CANDY: I have to leave in ten minutes; I gotta get out of town.
>
> PICKLES: I gotta get to work.
>
> ME: I have sex scheduled for 10 a.m.
>
> PICKLES: Oh, good. Have sex for all of us, won't you?
>
> ME: Triple orgasm, in honor of you both.
>
> AUNT CANDY: We appreciate that.
>
> PICKLES: Since I probably will never have sex again.
>
> AUNT CANDY: Or me, either. There's very little sex going on in *Vegas*. Don't you find that ironic?
>
> ME: I do. Now drink your coffee and let's pray for good travel, good work and good sex.

"A friend loves at all times and a sister is born for times of adversity." Proverbs 17:17

*Shari Simpson was a* BlogHer *'12 Voice of The Year in Humor which was terribly exciting until she realized she still had to clean her own toilets. She is the co-author of the comedy* Maybe Baby, It's You *(Dramatic Publishing, Inc.), the evil semi-genius behind the blog* Earth Mother just means I'm dusty, *writes for* In The Powder Room *and* Cool Mom Picks, *and creates and performs in comedy videos for* NickMom. *Shari is devoted to her church, bemused husband, three children (two human, one pug), and her crazy Italian mother. Oh, and Pickles and Aunt Candy. Of course. Connect with her on Twitter @DustyEarthMom.*

# A Pipeline Runs Through It

*by Tarja Parssinen*

At the beginning of any relationship—marital, gynecological, the waxing lady—things are so rosy, so full of breath mints and bladder control. A Dance of the Seven Veils, if you will: perfume, floss, concealer, thongs, and lies, lies, lies about a great many things. But veils are notoriously flimsy and the physical mystery falls away over the years, like an ever-widening bathroom door until one day, BAM, there you are having a conversation about mortgage rates while trimming your chin hairs.

Which brings me, of course, to the vapors. You know. Gas. I like using "the vapors" because it makes me feel very Scarlett O'Hara: "Oh, Ashley, I've got a case of the vapors!" (Movie retitled: *Gone with the Breaking Wind.*)

There was a time, however, when I was a zero emissions vehicle. The only one in my family. A cross-country family road trip in the mid-1990s, for example, was termed The Double-Bacon Cheeseburger and resulted in the near-asphyxiation of everyone in our minivan, as well as a schnauzer 50 feet away. Courts ruled that my brother was to blame. And quite possibly my father. With help from my sister. But I was innocent, I tell you!

Until that fateful day when an incision was made in my abdomen and uterus and the Jaws of Life ripped a 7 lb. 11 oz. chunk of joy out of me. At first, I blamed breastfeeding: "No spinach salad for me! Roughage equals fartage." People assumed I was just speaking about the baby. Then I blamed it on a fairly complex algorithm involving hormones, sleep-deprivation and sugar binges. But no matter what, gas was passed.

I was no longer the cute, environmentally friendly Prius. I was the ancient Chevy who never passed the smog-check. Global warming is real, my friends. And it's sleeping with my husband.

I had to ask tough questions like: "Is 'Caesarean section' Pig Latin for 'One Woman Fart Party'?" but I knew even without Googling it that when your body is opened up like that and your innards are tugged and pulled and jostled and tugged and pulled, it ain't never gonna be the same. The tectonic plates of your body are shifting, trying desperately to fit back together again in the face of pelvic floor spreading, incontinental drift, and increased volcanic activity. Your landmass is no longer a wonderland. It's a whoopee cushion.

And when a natural gas discovery is found off your ass-west coast, it becomes very difficult to control such explosive, er . . . power. It's best to run that pipeline straight to This-Is-Not-My-Body and tap that well in Ravaged-By-Child-Bearing. Because you're a public company, sister, and your stock ticker reads "MOM." In the face (or butt) of such odds, the physical mystery of relationships doesn't stand a chance. Gas is not sexy. Especially from women.

The injustice of it all is that society expects women to overshare verbally—you did WHAT with WHOM on a TRAMPOLINE?!—and men to overshare physically—Jim, dear, that's enough with the Bush's baked beans. But switch the equation up—Heavens to Betsy a lady TOOTED!—and you're playing with methane.

For example, I grew up in a very overshare-traditional household. By which I mean that my father left nothing to the imagination: he passed gas from the North and the South, quite proudly and with great humor. *That is what a man does!* I believed.

Except not my man. In a stunning turn of events, I married a man who continues—after 12 years together—to maintain every aspect of decorum and physical mystery. To top it all off, he closes the bathroom door. I was very confused for the first few years of our relationship. And burdened. I mean, his end of the veil was firmly intact, while mine was left flapping in the wind. Literally.

It is difficult and embarrassing for me to accept that through injury and childbirth and just not caring, I am preserving a family tradition—nobody light a match!—for future generations. And here I was thinking I would be passing along my father's bird's nest spaghetti recipe—so disappointing!

What has led me to this fateful (fartful) time in my life?

I can pinpoint the exact moment that my dignity left the building: spring, 2007. With my orthopedic surgeon. It was just the two of us. And by "two of us," I mean me and him and his surgical team. I wore the finest in one-ply paper towels, the lighting was dimmed to a blinding fluorescence. He took my leg gently, a questioning look in his eye. "Yes, that's the one," I told him. And then, either because he didn't believe me or wanted to re-enact a one-legged Tour de France, he did a final check to make sure they would be operating on the correct knee, by moving my leg in a bicycle motion, round and round, the paper towel up by my stomach, my hoo-haw bidding howdy to the crowd. Again. And again. And again.

The mystery was gone from my relationship with the surgeon, but it was a "Look, kids, Big Ben!" moment that would *surely* never be relived—and certainly not with anyone I knew personally.

And yet how do you recover gracefully from knee surgery in front of your fiancé without a colossal lack of dignity? Being unable to walk to the toilet or sit down on it by myself, I can tell you that it is done with no dignity whatsoever:

*Oh, you dear, sweet man who just asked me to marry him, please lower me slowly on the toilet, slowly, OW! GODDAMN IT! I SAID SLOWLY! Now just sit there and watch me while I do my business—don't go anywhere because you must now raise me up, gently, gently, GODDAMN IT! I SAID GENTLY! And, honey? I know it's 3 a.m. but I need to go to the bathroom again. Right now. Don't give me that look. You put a ring on it.*

One small, painful step to the bathroom, one giant leap toward a total lack of marital mystery. And in between? The cervical fluid, mucous plug, Tucks medicated wipes, hormones, Spanx, tears, lies, more tears, more lies, THAT IS NOT A PUSH-UP BRA, until finally, finally—making itself known in fits and starts (sits and farts)—a natural gas discovery.

Love is a thing of beauty, binding two people together in one mystical, magical land. A land where a river of respect runs through it and sometimes a pipeline, too.

There is a moment in the movie *This Is 40* where the wife asks her husband, "Can't we keep just a little bit of mystery in our relationship?"

Best of luck with that.

*Tarja grew up in Saudi Arabia and moved back to the States when she was 15. After earning her degree from Cornell University and performing with the sketch comedy group The Skits-O-Phrenics, she moved to New York City and worked at The Ad Council and Random House Publishing. In 2006, she moved to the Bay Area with her husband, where she launched two baby boys (now four and one) and a writing career. Tarja's work has appeared in various magazines and humor sites, on NPR, and at her website,* The Flying Chalupa, *where she strives to have a voice. A voice that doesn't have to count to three. Connect with her on Twitter @TheFlyingChlupa.*

# The Last Nice Jewish Boy in Boston

*by Anna Sandler*

When I was young and single and much prettier than I realized, I lived in Boston in a smaller-than-small apartment, and in between my mediocre job and late nights out with my best friends that we insisted were "inspired" instead of "insanely drunken," I dated every Jewish boy in Boston.

How do I know I dated *every single one?* Because despite it being the 1990s, which meant there was barely an Internet let alone a Google with which to "Google it," or in my case, "Google *him*," my mediocre job was doing data analysis in the market research department of a large Jewish organization that not only prided itself on having an exhaustive record of every Beantown Member of the Tribe, but had coded these individuals by gender, age and marital status. Intent on finding my nice Jewish husband before I turned 30, I ran a report of every single Jewish guy between the ages of 26-30 who had an address within the Boston city limits.

And then, with each bad blind date, Jewish mixer gone awry, and drunken bar meeting, I crossed every name from Avi and Ari to Zack and Zev off my list until eventually after four years there wasn't a single name that had not been indelibly struck-through with my black Sharpie.

When the last Jacob had been dispatched for showing up 20 minutes late for our third date, followed by taking me to a bar *I didn't even like*, and then proceeding to talk way too much about the nervous disposition of his Dalmatian puppy, which I should add we had already discussed in great detail on our two previous dates, I immediately called my brother in Manhattan.

"Guess who's moving to New York?!" I exclaimed happily.

"Why?" Came his too-quick reply to my riddle.

"There's no one left to date in Boston," I sigh-whined.

"Stop, that's ridiculous. You just feel that way after a few bad dates. You don't need to write-off an entire town just because some guy named Josh may or may not talk too much about his dog."

"First, his name is Jacob and not Josh. At least you should misremember it as Joshua, if he's not a Jake he's certainly not a Josh. Anyway, it doesn't matter because I'm never seeing him again. And secondly, he didn't talk *too much* about his dog—he *only* talked about his dog. And it wasn't even a very cute dog. Maybe some tales about a cute little pug or some dog like that, I could listen to, but Dalmatian stories? No thank you."

"All I'm trying to say," my brother continued in his carefully patient I'm-the-big-brother voice, "is that of course you don't need to move to New York because you feel like there's no one left to date in Boston. It's not like you live in some small town in Iowa. It's Boston, there are plenty of guys just, uh, dying to go out with a ni- well, maybe not nice . . . *fun* girl like you."

"I don't think you understand," I said in my carefully patient do-not-patronize-the-little-sister voice, "I do data analysis for a living. I have a printout from work listing all the single Jewish men in Boston between the ages of 26-30. I've actually, factually dated them all. Even your sort-of friend from college who you said I wouldn't like—did you know I totally went out with him? We went to that place with the really strong drinks on Claremont Park. It was hilarious. Becca was at the bar, and then I gave her a secret signal just like out of the movies and she just joined us out of nowhere and stayed for the rest of the date. He had no idea what to say, but honestly I couldn't stand another minute. By the way? You were so right. He is like the definition of bo-ring. And he makes way too many hand gestures when he talks. What's up with that?"

"You know he has a brother."

"Of course I know he has a brother! And in retrospect, I think I might have liked him more—his work history is very interesting, and he participated in our community service day three years in a row, but you know I have a 'No Dating the Brother' policy."

"I did not know that."

"Of course. I'm classy like that."

"Of course."

"So you can see why I need to move to New York."

"Yes, it's perfectly clear now. And I think you'll love it in New York. The futon's ready when you are. I'll warn, I mean *tell* my roommate."

But I didn't really mean it. Despite having exhausted every possible date in town, I had my job and my girl gang, and perhaps most significantly, inertia.

I liked my teeny-tiny single girl apartment, my ladies-only gym and the familiarity of my job, even if it was mediocre. I liked that there were bars where I was a regular and restaurants that didn't say a word when I ordered my usual bacon, horseradish and avocado sandwich.

The next day while I was at work, contemplating my entire future, the phone rang. As it was 1999, I actually took the call.

"Hello!"

"Hey, it's Becca. I have a set-up for you. Like a *good* set-up."

"Becca, you don't. You know that I know that you don't. You can't. It's not possible."

"Ha, ha. Yeah, I don't know how he ever managed to stay off your grid, but it's true. He's cute, he's single, and he's tall. He's Jewish. Oh and he drives a nice car."

"Becca, you know I don't care about cars, I'm not shallow. Tell me more about his height."

"Well," Becca thought before answering, "he's very tall, but not creepy, gangly tall. You would totally like him. You *will* totally like him. He's not that funny, though. And I think he might be a Republican."

"Eh, whatever. I can deal with that. Hold on, what's his name? I'll pull up his record," I said as I closed the door to my office, just in case my boss didn't think the organization's confidential database should be used for my own personal dating service. (I will note for the record, that at the time online dating was just beginning, so in a way I was really ahead of my time despite my 1950s-ish husband-seeking ways.)

Becca said, not unkindly, "You do know it's possible for there to be a Nice Jewish Boy who's not on your list?"

"I do know it's *possible*, and also that it's very *unlikely*. Keeping people on the grid is my job, and I am very good at my job, thankyouverymuch. What's his name again?"

Becca gave me his name, I typed it in, and instantly as the computer returned his record in green type against a black background I knew the tall, dull Jew was not going to happen.

"I told you no one stays off my grid! Nope, this is a no go. He's living with someone. Coded partner and a single address for him and some girl."

Becca continued, "He and I work together. He was telling us the whole story today at lunch, they were living together but she moved out."

"Moved out how? Like home to her parents in Medford but they're going to get back together? Or moved in with three friends in Central Square but just until she and the guy work things out?"

"No, not like that at all. Like moved to Detroit with her new boyfriend."

"Wow, I almost feel sorry for her. Who moves to Detroit?" I wondered.

"I know!" Becca replied. "I don't think I even know anyone from Detroit, let alone anyone who would move there and become someone from Detroit."

We sat in silence for a moment, contemplating a parallel life of unknown boyfriends who were good enough that you would leave your perfectly nice, tall, Republican boyfriend in Boston. I pictured the new guy with a motorcycle, wry graphic tees and an infectious smile. Suddenly her rejected boyfriend in Boston seemed more than good enough for me.

"Well, if there really isn't anyone else in the picture . . . "

"I promise," Becca said, "there really isn't. I'll give him your number and tell him to call."

"Thanks. It's really too bad I'm not allowed to re-code marital status, because you know I don't like the idea of dating someone who isn't officially an S in the database."

"I know," Becca agreed, "but sometimes it's the exception that proves the rule."

Mike Sandler and I went on our first date a few weeks later, when I happily found out that he was as cute and tall as advertised, and thankfully, neither dull nor a Republican.

Two years later to the day Mike and I got married in New York City.

And that is how on the eve of the millennium I met my husband, the very last single Jew in Boston, age 26-30.


*Anna Sandler is a writer and mom living happily ever after in scenic New Jersey with her charming husband and three delightful children. Anna blogs about motherhood and mayhem on* RandomHandprints.com *and shares husband humor on the Facebook page,* Instructions for my Husband. *Anna is a regular contributor to* New Jersey Family *magazine and* The Huffington Post, *and was selected as a 2013* BlogHer *Humor Voice of the Year. She wants you to know that a few details of this story have been exaggerated, as they should be in any good Bubbe Meise (tall tale). Connect with her on Twitter @Anna_Sandler.*

# The Gym: A Place Where Muscles and Gag Reflexes Go to Workout

*by Tracy Winslow*

The warm water cascades down my back. Inhaling the wonderful scent of rosemary mint, the stress of my day begins to rinse away with the shampoo bubbles. Ignorant to the dangers lurking outside, I reach for the body wash. Suddenly the plastic curtain is yanked open. I gag as my heart drop kicks my uvula. I am armed with only a Venus and am planning my next move as I hear my attacker say . . .

"Yeah, I left my face wash in there. Can I have it?"

Alas, this is not the Bates Motel. I am in the gym locker room and sticking your arm in a stranger's shower is commonplace behavior here.

On the tour of your new gym facility you are shown the pool, spa, sauna, workout and yoga rooms. You are provided with a schedule of classes, a towel, and the option for a personal trainer to kick your ass into shape. The astronomical membership fee includes: beautiful mirrors, hair dryers, fluffing and puffing condiments such as Q-tips, deodorant, hair spray—everything down to the delicious cucumber infused water to quench your parched post-workout esophagus. What they fail to give you is a warning about the WOMEN who frequent the locker room.

There are three types of ladies at the gym: the "hide in the bathroom stall to get ready" type, the "change quickly and go about your business" type, and the "I secretly believe that I may be asked to be in porn and therefore need to flaunt my nudity—so feast your eyes on this garden of love" type.

I grew up embracing the Puritan belief of "no one needs to see your naked ass so put that shit away." You enter the locker room, you exhibit some modesty getting ready and you get the fuck out. There should be minimal eye contact, conversation, or time spent changing. However, I have yet to see this mantra embroidered onto couch pillows here on the West Coast. My virgin eyeballs were in for quite a shock when I moved to Flap-Your-Floobs-In-My-Face*, California (*not its real name).

Now, if I looked like a Victoria's Secret model I'd probably be naked all the time. People would be like *"Tracy, it's thirty-seven freakin' degrees outside. Why are you wearing a bikini and high heels at Stop and Shop?"* And clearly my answer would be *"It may be cold outside but I don't feel it because I'm hot."* I might even crack a walnut with my ass, or something equally impressive with my hotness.

However, the movie star body doubles are never the naked ones. The naked ones are always rockin' boobs that could be used as sand bags in the case of a flood. They could start a fire with their thighs if they ran fast enough. They could fashion a burka out of their excess stomach skin. Now, for the record, there's absolutely nothing wrong with the way their bodies look. *(Says the girl wearing an outfit that could double as a couch slipcover).* I just don't need to get an in-depth visual inspection of someone's love muffin while I'm trying to find a pair of socks.

I want to grab them by their naked shoulders and shake them while asking *"What the hell makes you want to lie spread eagle in a lounge chair someone dragged in from the pool? Is wearing clothing so unbearably constricting that you can't possibly relax without giving everyone a tour of your salt-and-pepper cooch? For the love of all that is holy—at least place this towel over your honey pot—it's included in your monthly dues!"*

Also dry-heave inducing is the pre-workout butt-naked stretching. There needs to be a plaque that states the following:

*Dear Naked Patrons of this Very Expensive Gym:*

*I can't help but notice you prancing around naked as a jaybird—as I almost lost an eye the other day to a cold nipple. While this may be acceptable behavior at the Playboy Bunny Mansion, or at band camp—here at Very Expensive Gym it makes many of us vomit copiously in our mouths. Please be advised that stretching out your thighs while nude is NOT attractive. Same for naked limbering up your backs, chests and core before Zumba which, in fact, crosses the line into horrifying. Skyclad calisthenics are creepy. Don't you worry about a spider or who-knows-what crawling up into your hoo-ha from prior naked sitter-uppers?*

*Additionally, please put your downward facing dog ass somewhere else out of my line of vision. Preferably not on the bench where I plan to sit (fully clothed) to lace up my Nike Shox.*

*Thank you for your adherence to an iota of societal discretion.*

*Signed,*

*The Slightly Self-Conscious People Trying To Change Without Sweaty Vagina Nightmares All Up In Our Mix*

It took me a little while to learn how to retch silently at the visual assault scorched into my retinas every step to, and from, the showers. You have to focus on your pedicure or witness a buffet of fried egg boobs. I don't think everyone should shower in scuba gear. Neither do I wish to converse about the weather with a woman scratching her episiotomy scar. Also some things should be done with privacy like: tampon insertion, nose hair deforestation or bringing yourself to orgasm while cleaning your ears with a Q-tip (as a side note—how *do* you do that because I'd totally pay extra for that class).

It's awkward enough to try to squeeze out of a sweaty spandex straitjacket while trying to hide my deflated-condom-post-baby stomach. I DON'T want to talk about Lindsay Lohan and her fucktillionth arrest, with the person drying off every hirsute millimeter with a cotton ball. Plus, when I'm uncomfortable embarrassing things tend to escape my mouth like: *"Tell your beaver to watch out for splinters while it's gnawing on that bench."* Which makes ME look like I'm the weird one, instead of the naked woman giving herself a leisurely pedicure on the counter.

Once out of the shower, and in an attempt to find a location for modest costume changes where Assasaurus Rex isn't around to hip check me, I retreat to the farthest ends of the locker room. I'm drying my hair when a woman comes in from the showers. She drops her towel, palms a handful of boobage and begins to use the hairdryer to dry beneath her cleavage, abdomen, and arm pits. (*Note to self: bring a hairdryer from home*).

The girl with the driest boobs on the block then hikes her left leg up, placing her foot on the edge of the counter. She then picks the hair dryer back up and *I SHIT YOU NOT*—begins to coif her vajayjay *with a hairbrush*. And just when I think her behavior can't possibly get any more bizarre—*she hairsprays her cha cha*. No, she didn't mistakenly grab Tigi Bed Head thinking she was giving herself a deodorant rosebush. She read the bottle before she began spraying those little bastards into sticky submission and then finished off the job with a motherfucking barrette.

And, because I am like a discreet ninja—she catches me gawking at her and my jaw getting rug burn from hitting the ground. Classy as ever, I blurt the first thing that comes to mind: "Wow. Fancy! Would you like a spritz of my Chanel Chance to finish off the vag prep?" Shockingly, she does not take me up on my enticing offer for a high-end tunnel of love. Because, apparently *that* would be weird.

Using a Venus in the shower to create a heart shaped box as opposed to tweezing while waiting in line for a protein shake is clearly gauche in Twiddle-Your-Twat-In-My-Face*, California (*also not its real name). So I think I need to take a class on naked gym etiquette. Maybe the scary boot camp instructor can incorporate a few of these lessons into her class. Although...naked burpees? I wonder if my membership fees cover damages resulting from the aftershocks of a naked stomach tsunami . . .

*Tracy Winslow is a SAHM trying not to raise a flock of assholes. Besides crafting cocktails with Zoloft, Tracy can be found cursing, crying into her coffee over her stretch marks, and Ouija-boarding her deceased metabolism. She was voted one of the Top 25 Funniest Moms of 2013 at* Circle of Moms/PopSugar. *Tracy is a weekly staff writer for* In The Powder Room *and a regular contributor to* Families in the Loop, Mamas Against Drama, The Epistolarians, *and* Mamapedia. *When she's not trying to Brillo the image of naked hoo-has from her cerebellum, she can be found blogging at* Momaical.com *and Twatting @Momaical.*

# Confessions of a Craft Hater

*by Kim Forde*

The whole thing started innocently enough.

I knew I didn't belong there—but I was desperate, out of options. They had something I needed. Something I had tried to find elsewhere and couldn't. What else was I supposed to do?

And, so, with massive trepidation, I went in. I knew it would be ugly. I knew I was taking a huge chance on my ability to hold it together.

I knew my limits and I knew the mental tricks I had to play with myself to get through this.

*Stay focused. Know my route. Get in and get out.*

Once inside, I had my eyes set on my destination. As I feared, it was all the way across the room, with many obstacles to cross. But I steadied my resolve.

I was OK at first.

But it wasn't long before my anxiety crept in, slowly building. *I'm out of place. Not like everyone else here. They all know. They're looking at me. They can sense how lost I am.*

I lost my focus and that's where everything started to unravel.

I looked at the signs above me. They were triggers, every one of them.

**Apparel Crafting**
**Art Supplies**
**Bakeware**
**Beads**
**Craft Painting**
**Floral**
**Framework**
**Home Decor**
**Scrapbooking**
**Seasonal**
**Wedding**
**Yarn & Needle Crafts**

I felt like I was getting the shakes. I attempted to put one foot in front of the other. *I just need one item. I just need one item.*

Repeat and walk. Repeat and walk.

And then, in the periphery, creeping ever closer to the center of my field of vision, there they were. The fake flowers. And the teeny-tiny little scrapbooking pieces. And the woodworking section and the baking and the sewing and the jewelry making—ohmygod it's fucking dizzying.

I was vaguely aware of the others and how content they appeared, perusing one tiny-ass piece of some such thing after another.

I reached a tipping point, one I had felt before. One where I felt like I needed air, or possibly medication. Like I needed to be steadied. Like I needed—HOLY SHIT, WHERE IS THE EXIT? I'M

SWEATING, ALL I SEE ARE TINY PIECES OF PLASTIC—FUCK, I JUST GOT A PLASTIC FLOWER IN MY EYE! WHERE IS THE FUCKING EXIT?

\* \* \*

OK, so I won't be buying baking supplies in the craft store anymore. Well, I can't, technically, for 180 days, according to my lawyer. People get so fucking touchy over one public meltdown. No patrons were hurt, so what's the big deal? They were all safely hiding behind the garden gnomes, clutching their homemade lucky charms and hurling variety packs of pipe cleaners at me.

Well, that's how I remember it. But "the public record" just makes me sound like I lost my shit in the craft store.

Potato, potahto.

I just don't craft.

I probably never will.

And I am strangely fascinated by those who do. By this, I mean I am sort of scared of you crafters.

You guys with the key fob club passes to Michaels. And Jo-Ann Fabrics. And A.C. Moore.

You guys with the craft rooms in your house.

Yeah, you. I'm a little scared of you.

It's not my fault. It's genetic. I come from a long line of non-crafters. My mom doesn't have the DIY gene and neither did her mom. I never sat home as a kid longing for a sewing kit or an afternoon of mosaic creations. I did enjoy those pre-packaged pot-holder looming kits once in a blue moon, but that's about it.

And now? As a mom? Yeah, still not crafting. Books? Check. Toys? Of course. Outdoor play? We're there. But you'll never find me spreading out an assortment of sticks, pinecones, glue and glitter for a rainy day project. I'm not building dioramas or getting my spare Popsicle sticks together for cabin assembly.

And the craft rooms? Can we talk about those for a minute?

Look, you have enough crafting supplies that you need a full room in your house to store your stuff? OK, I respect your dedication and commitment—seriously, I do. I'm just thinking about all those trips to the craft store that it took to set up that room. And of course that gives me the fucking shakes again.

Truth be told, I'm also thinking about what else I could do with a spare room in my house. Here are a few of the possibilities that come to mind:

## A Wine Room

Obviously. If you have an extra room in your house that deserves a dedicated purpose, I just fail to understand how wine does not win here by a landslide of seismic proportions.

## A Cheese Cave

I mean, if we're thinking out loud here, and you, for some reason, can't get behind the wine room, then a domestic artisanal haven where I can chip away at walls of aged gorgonzola with my teeth— at my leisure—would be an acceptable runner-up.

## A Panic Room

For moms. You know, secretly hidden in the house—so that I have a place away from my kids where I can store and eat my top-secret- not-fucking-sharing-with-the-under-6-set-ice-cream-stash in peace. Complete with soundproof doors and a trap door breezeway to aforementioned wine room.

But hey, if you want to store gift-wrap from hanging industrial rolls and 76 variations of tiny cutout stars in an elaborate-yet-satisfying-to-you filing system, I seriously have no right to judge you. Not for a minute. Especially when my main hobby entails oversharing my life on the Internet in the form of a blog with about 12 readers.

Who am I to mock you for your scrapbooking, your mosaic making or your looming? If you're not a deviant who is storing jars of human fingernail clippings under your bed, then craft away, my friends.

I just can't join you. I would love to understand you. I would love to compare notes and show off my efforts all over Pinterest. But, deep down, I have no desire to own a glue gun. And I think that the texture of felt is downright creepy.

What about my kids, you ask? Well, early indicators show mixed results on their genetic crafting deficiencies. My son is just like me. Or maybe he's just like many boys, with no real interest in coloring, cutting, gluing or the like. But I have all the supplies—OK, the basic ones—here at his disposal if he changes his mind.

My daughter, on the other hand, may prove to derail this streak with the coloring and painting. That's OK—I won't stand in her way.

I'm keenly aware of how her ears perk up when we visit her friends for a playdate and their moms say, "Do you want to do a craft?"

The words hit her like a foreign language. She looks almost confused by the bin of options that is made available to her. She looks at me and I nod in approval: *Go for it.* And I wonder how long until glitter, mini-stars and the like will completely infiltrate my house and undo the very core of my non-crafting being.

If (when) this happens—I ask, as my daughter cuts snowflakes beside me—will I need to buy color-coded bins? Drawers of multiple sizes? A filing system? How do you keep all of the paper organized and the five million tiny little pieces of Crafting Hell from taking over your house?

How?

You will all have to show me. Maybe even at the craft store. Someday.

After the restraining order is lifted.

*Kim Forde writes about the art of perfecting domestic failure on her blog,* The Fordeville Diaries. *A former NYC resident, she now is a secret suburban convert at home with her three young kids, managing her Starbucks addiction and healthy fear of craft stores. Kim has written for several parenting and humor blogs, and was recognized as a 2013 Humor Voice of the Year by BlogHer. She is also a contributor to the best-selling anthology,* I Just Want to Pee Alone, *and recently appeared in the New York City production of* Listen to Your Mother. *Armed with a keyboard and an addiction to storytelling, she spends more time on blogging and social media than she's prepared to admit. Connect with her on Twitter @Fordeville.*

# Love and Other Drugs

*by Bethany Thies*

When I was 15, I had my very first sip of alcohol. It burned. Not as much as my love for the boy next to me, but enough to warrant a moment of mild reflection. Even at that age, I questioned my ability to see my path through the thrill. What we were doing was wrong. It was dangerous, but it was exhilarating. I was an actor in a matinee playing to a different kind of packed theatre. I had the luxury of having no one to blame for my mistakes aside from the people trying their hardest to protect me. I had no sense of my own mortality or the weight of belonging to my parents. With these perfectly formed untruths, I stumbled on. The greatest of all my mistakes were the ones I made in the throes of "love."

In the beginning, it was the pull of infatuation. Then, infatuation would lead to a decision I would be unable to take back. Even later still, I would marry a man who loved me as little as I loved myself. And so on and so on it went, the seeking of truth and beauty while not believing it existed in me.

My framework was broken while I furiously attempted to build the add-on.

Looking back, I have always been heavily under the influence of love.

For years, I'd shamelessly reached out to grab a piece of the love pie, quickly inhaled its sweetness and, almost immediately, would feel the sickening fullness of eating something without substance.

For every short-lived high there was the inevitable and substantial low. Until the day I met my second husband, the man who would become the father of my children.

Very shortly after my husband and I met, I whispered across a smoke-filled room to my best friend, dressed in '70s hot pants, that, "I was going to have babies with him," complete with behind-the-back dramatic pointing in case she was unsure that I was talking about the man sitting directly next to me. It was the fake '70s; I needed to make things clear.

And, very shortly thereafter, we were engaged and pregnant with our first. We notified the family of our impending arrival at a Mother's Day brunch hosted in our dingy, east Hollywood apartment. Standing room only while a fight broke out in front of the building.

Eight weeks later, I stood at the altar of The Little Chapel of the West in Las Vegas staring at this man I high-dived into loving. Our closest friends, family and Elvis by our side. During the ceremony, the July sweat slowly made its way down my pregnant legs. What the hell were we doing? Was I going to vomit during our first married kiss? Were my breasts always going to be this big?

I was a second-time bride with a first-time, blushing groom and our first trimester baby along for the ride. My first marriage had ended kamikaze style less than a year earlier, after several years of imploding led to a pyrotechnics show you could see from Space. I give good explosion.

Only two Thanksgivings prior, I'd turned to my then husband (for the sake of story development, we'll call him..."Old Husband") and said, "I want to have a baby. What if we start trying next year?" and, on the beautiful deck of a gorgeous Northern California home on what was a perfect, picturesque weekend, we maybe-sorta-kinda agreed that we would possibly talk about it. The details, blurry, as there was not a dry liver in the house. That night, I walked outside, alone, to call my father with the idea of Motherhood inhabiting all the spaces left unfilled by turkey. Wandering down a dark road, with a million stars overhead, we discussed family, gratitude and assorted minutiae. The sky was so black, I couldn't see the outline of my own body against the night. In that moment, I felt connected. Part of the Earth I stood on, part of a relationship I thought was headed toward the logical next step, part of the league of anticipatory mothers-in-waiting everywhere, but mostly part of a phone call that reminded me that family would always be there; even in the darkest places where you couldn't quite find yourself.

Less than a year later, I left. I moved into a spare room in the never-mentioned-in-cinema San Fernando Valley. I was drinking too much. I was writing terrible poetry. I was starting over. I was afraid I would never find anything better than the bad I'd suddenly walked away from. I questioned everything.

While I mourned, I found myself always going back to that picturesque Thanksgiving weekend. Second-guessing my resolve. Second-guessing the small, wounded part of me that knew enough to leave. And in the forefront of all that, mourning the idea of a child created only in half-sober discussion and my mind.

But, in a Los Angeles January, wearing fake eyelashes and a belted jumpsuit, with a man I barely knew next to my side, fidgeting with his fake mustache, and a record player showcasing Shirley Bassey blaring in the background, I knew. This was it. I was going to have babies with him. It was ridiculous. It made absolutely no sense. It was perfect.

The following February, she was born. The ultimate grade A, uncut love. Love that put all other love to shame and in perspective. Love that I felt so deeply in my body that I would sit in bed at night choking back sobs of gratitude and fear. She was so perfect and I didn't deserve her. Then, something happened. Every day, little by little, her love started to heal the fractured pieces. And love became something different. It didn't have to be dangerous. It could be quiet. It could be peaceful. It could be raw, but, gentle. I loved her and she loved me. We were a family. Love no longer had to hurt to make sense.

Now, there are six of us at the table. And almost eight years later, no one has come down from the high. The girl I thought I was, the woman I am, the woman I want to be, the imperfect mother, the wife, the maker of promises and the believer in happy endings—I am still heavily under the influence of love.

*Bethany Thies is a writer and the proud mother to four young Vikings. She is the author of the parenting blog,* Bad Parenting Moments *and the chronically unread poetry blog,* Room for Cream. *She can often be found searching for socks, keys, discount non-perishables and a bathroom lock her children cannot pick. Bethany's work has been published on several parenting sites and, when they'll have her, in old-fashioned black and white in her local, independent newspaper. Her children are unimpressed. Connect with her on Twitter @BPMbadassmama.*

# My Masturbating Grandma

*by Angela Shelton*

If you don't think your grandma masturbates, you're wrong.

Did you just fall over? Can't get up? I totally understand.

Imagine me, a few years ago, sharing a typical Southern lunch with my grandmother, complete with biscuits, sliced 'maters, corn-on-the-cob, green beans and onions, when the topic of sex came up. There I was munching on a 'mater while my grandmother gnawed a line across her ear of corn, and stared at me. All of a sudden from across the table she spat out, with a few pieces of corn, "Ya ain't gonna be like yer Mama, are you? Marrying all them men."

I didn't know what to say to that. My mom is the black sheep of the family. That was already very understood. It was no secret I'd had my share of boyfriends too. I thought about reminding my grandmother that I had been married already and narrowly escaped that mess, but I didn't say anything. I just stared back at her, waiting, like watching a rattlesnake.

My grandmother could be as mean as a nest-poked hornet. The whole family knew that. Even though I was in my 30s, in her mind I wasn't too old to be switched. If you don't know what a switch is, you are not from the South. It's a freshly yanked branch from a tree, used just like a whip and hurts like one too. There was something about the way she held that corn-on-the-cob as she glared at me that kept me quiet.

After she finished mowing another line in her corn she continued with, "Men only want sex. That's all they want, is sex." She picked her teeth. I forked at the beans on my plate. What else do you do when your grandmother starts talking about sex?

"Uh, huh," I mumbled, just to see how far she was going with this.

"Men just want sex. All of them. That's all they want." She put her corn cob down. I totally wanted to ask her if she'd started dating in her 80s and had been dissed for not putting out. Instead I just stared at her with a slight grin as I chewed.

My grandmother was more open with me than any of her other grandchildren. I think it all went back to the time I cursed her out in the middle of the family reunion. I was eight-years-old and about to get switched for something I didn't do, when I put my hands on my hips and said every bad word I'd ever heard in my short life, even made up some as I yelled at her to stop beating us. I ordered her to never lay a hand on me again. She never did either. I had gained her respect.

As I grew up, my grandmother was always nicer to me than she was to my mom. She even came to stay with me in New York City in my loft apartment for her 70th birthday. We got tipsy on white wine, which I'm not allowed to talk about, on the Circle Line boat tour. She confessed how she'd never wanted to be married in the first place. Never wanted kids either. She'd wanted to be a painter. In her semi-drunken state she urged me to always follow my dreams and never let a man hold me back for nothing.

Sitting at the lunch table, I decided to push the sex conversation. "Gran, everyone wants sex. I want sex," I said, sliding back in my chair just in case her long arm came around to smack me.

She lowered her corn cob and stared at me. I thought twice about egging her on and made sure both of my feet were square on the floor, ready for a dart towards the door. I scooped up a mouthful of green beans while she eyeballed me.

She huffed in a breath of air and said matter-of-factly, "Well, get into the shower with a soapy washcloth and take care of it then."

Yep, that's what she said. *Get into the shower with a soapy washcloth and take care of it then.* While that visual burned into my brain, my mouthful of beans shot out across the table. I swear I could see the corners of my grandmother's mouth turn up in a grin which she tried to hide. She was entertained.

Once I composed myself, and made sure I wasn't going to choke to death, I summoned up my courage and asked, "Is that what you do?"

She looked at me for a moment. Her grin went straight and she looked away and said, "Have a biscuit."

I stared at her in shock and awe as I reached for a warm biscuit. My grandmother masturbated with a washcloth. For the life of me, I could not figure out how you could do that. Like how, literally, did you use a washcloth? I choked up, covering a laugh two more times, once on a 'mater and once on a piece of ice from the sweet tea. My grandmother caught my eye each time and just said, "Now." Her way of telling me to behave; washcloths weren't that big a deal—men only wanting sex was!

We ate in silence, stealing glances at each other, trying to keep our grins forced down.

Then later, in the shower, I saw it. It had been hanging there for my entire life, but I had never thought it could be used for...and I never looked at it in the same way again. You know when you buy a bag of onions at the grocery store, how they come in that mesh bag? Well, in the South you don't spend money on things like expensive loofahs like city folk do, so you make your own. You take one of those onion bags, put a bar of Ivory soap in the middle and tie a knot on either side. Then you tie knots on the very ends, making a handle on each side. There, you have yourself a fancy loofah to scrub your back. Or if you folded a washcloth around the soap, you could have one hell of a handy contraption . . .

Showering at my grandmother's house was forever altered. No, I never used her onion bag, but I would stand there, washing my hair, staring at it. Then I would try and wash the idea of my grandmother masturbating out of my head, like she washed away her urges.

Now that my grandmother has passed away, I often think of the things she taught me. By cursing her out I learned the power of standing up and protecting yourself. From our secret drunken night on the boat, circling Manhattan, I learned to always follow your dreams so you don't have regrets on your 70th birthday. From our little sex talk over 'mater biscuits, I learned that you're never too old to get into the shower with a soapy washcloth and take care of it.

Bless your heart, Gran.

*Angela Shelton is an acclaimed filmmaker, author, actor and public speaker. Her multi-award winning film* Searching for Angela Shelton *put a spotlight on sexual abuse and domestic violence and began a grassroots movement of healing for abuse survivors worldwide. Angela has appeared on* The Oprah Winfrey Show, Larry King Live, 48 Hours Investigates, NPR, Lifetime Television for Women, The Ricki Lake Show, *and the cover of the* New York Times. *She now lives in the country, married to her first love, and is fulfilling her dream of writing books in a barn house while still doing her service work. Come visit* AngelaShelton.com *and find out more about her life, including how she's following her grandmother's advice, and connect with Angela on Twitter @AngelaShelton.*

# Why Going to the DMV and the Gynecologist Are Basically the Same Thing

*by Lisa Newlin*

There are many responsibilities women have that are less than desirable. However, there are a few annual tasks that are especially heinous. No, I'm not talking about anal, but that's an excellent guess. I'm talking about going to the DMV and the gynecologist, although all three tasks undoubtedly involve crying and the application of ointment afterwards.

Going to the DMV is a necessary evil, but that doesn't make it any less horrible. I had to go recently, and as I stood there judging others silently, I realized going to the DMV is similar to going to the lady doctor. In case you don't follow my logic on the obvious connection, here are a few reasons why:

**1. You wait until the last minute to go,** because both are miserable experiences. It's only when you're on the verge of getting ticketed and fined do you begin the dreaded trek to the DMV.

Similarly, with the gyno, you only make the appointment when you're on your last pack of birth control pills and your little angel draws a mural on your dining room wall of you and daddy "washing each other" in the shower. Nothing like a little reminder in crayon that those tiny pills are necessary. Appointment made.

**2. You feel violated when you leave.** Nearly everyone can agree that going to either place is an unpleasant experience. No one looks forward to either event as a fun way to spend a Saturday. I'm sure there are those who would enjoy the experience, but they're currently locked on a psychiatric floor getting the much-needed help and treatment they deserve.

Normally, accomplishing a dreaded task leaves you feeling fulfilled and excited. Checking something off the to-do list is invigorating, especially when it involves a task you're less enthused about, like grocery shopping or snuggling with your husband. (Maybe that last one is just something I hate.)

But for some reason, leaving both the DMV and the gyno makes you want to throw on a chastity belt and close the entrance to the fun zone forever. The DMV makes you want to deny access because of the strange people you saw there—and nothing clamps up your cooter more than a one-handed man with two teeth trying to scratch his crotch while holding onto his driver's license. The gyno makes you want to deny access to your love box simply because you fear you picked up the clap while waiting to see the doctor.

Actually, getting the clap is another valid fear about going to the DMV. Tests are pending.

**3. You don't want to touch anything.** Whether it's the DMV or the gyno, touching anything without sterilizing yourself both before and after the contact is a death wish. Both places are equally covered in DNA and excrement from the orifices of people I'd rather not think about.

Don't worry. Alcohol is a sterilizing agent, so bring that with you. Vodka is my cleaner of choice.

**4. There's a weird smell.** I have a fairly good guess as to what causes the odd odor at the gynecologist, but I'm at a loss as to what causes the funky smell at the DMV. I suspect it's a combination of sweat and body odor lightly masked by the faint perfume of a pine-scented car air freshener.

Come to think of it, that's the same smell at the gynecologist.

**5. There's never anyone attractive there (except for you, of course).** I've never seen good-looking people at either of these venues, which is a disappointment because at least having eye candy to gaze upon makes the wait a little less painful. No such luck.

When I'm in the waiting room at the gyno, I don't want to see people who make me dry heave at the thought of them in the adjoining room, stripping off with nothing but a Bounty paper towel draped delicately over their happy town. (For many of these women, I'd say their happy town has been deserted for some time.)

I'm not a vagina expert, but if a woman can't manage to brush her teeth regularly, I suspect her lady parts are in severe disarray, if she can even find her lady parts among what is sure to be a dense forest.

The same holds true for the DMV, as far as the lack of good-looking people. I don't know when attractive people take care of their state motor vehicle needs, but it definitely isn't on the days I go.

**6. You need to prepare before arriving.** As if going through with these appointments isn't bad enough, both require preparation ahead of time, so not only does it ruin your day, it ruins the day before as well.

Whether it's gathering your tax documents and proof of insurance, or gathering your grooming utensils and trimming a smiley face into your pubic patch, both trips require an element of planning before walking through the doors. You can only hope one of them results in an appreciation of your efforts.

**7. You leave with less money than you arrived with, and all you want to do when you leave is burn your clothes.** This one really is self-explanatory, as it's simple math. You go, you pay, you get violated in some way, and then you leave. It's kind of like visiting a prostitute, but without the affection and nuzzling.

Perhaps the worst part about going to either locale is that you don't just have to endure the experience, but that you have to pay for it too. Most things in life you pay for are things you desire, such as a house or a movie. But the DMV and the gyno both strap you down and force you to pay for their services, regardless of whether you want them or not. One of them does so literally, the other figuratively.

Come to think of it, the gynecologist has it all worked out. What better way to ensure someone pays a bill than to strap them down to a freezing cold table covered loosely with grey plastic, have them remove their clothes and don a dinner napkin, and then make them spread their legs?

And isn't that just what the DMV feels like? At least there you get to wear clothing, although whatever you wear will be burned as soon as you exit the building.

So there you have it—visiting the gyno and going to the DMV are basically the same thing. But even though both experiences are similar, make sure you're at least somewhat conscious when you go to each. Slamming a shot of vodka can indeed take the edge off, but you don't want to get so blitzed that you get confused about where you are. It would be embarrassing to strip naked at the DMV and put your legs around the photo machine, thinking they're the stirrups at the gyno. I suspect the photo that would emerge isn't what you want on your driver's license either—especially if you're having a bad hair day.

Equally awkward would be going to the gyno and asking him if your "tags" are expired. You may not want to know the answer to that question.

Pay attention to where you are and be aware of the similarities and you will be fine. The last thing you want to do is embarrass yourself in front of the one-handed man with two teeth trying to scratch his crotch while holding onto his driver's license. He'll have a hard enough time doing your gynecological examination with only one hand.

*Lisa is a humor blogger who plays an unconvincing lawyer in real life. She shouldn't be allowed around sharp objects, anything breakable, or anything with carbohydrates. She prefers dogs over most people, and food over most everything. Her blog, LisaNewlin.com will make you feel better about your own life and remind you that vodka is the answer to everything. Except if the question is "What should I throw on this fire?" Then the answer is definitely NOT vodka. Connect with her on Twitter @Lisa_Newlin.*

# Head Games

*by Suzanne Fleet*

I met him at a Christmas party . . . tall and nerdy-cute with floppy brown hair.

When he told me he was an accountant, I cringed visibly. He laughed and said, "I'm an accountant at work and a break dancer in da club," demonstrating with, of all things, a busted version of the robot. And so he was in.

Being single in the modern era isn't easy. What qualifies as "seeing someone" is usually just a text, like: "You going out tonight? Let's hook-up later."

So I was impressed that, instead of playing head games with me like most of the guys I knew, Mark called and asked me out on a formal date the next day. He didn't even pull the *Swingers* thing and make me sweat it out for a few days.

This, I knew, was a sign that he actually liked me and was interested in more than a little wham-bam-thank-you-ma'am.

I started pondering the important questions. Like if I should buy a new outfit.

When Saturday finally rolled around, I started getting ready way too early—painting a mud mask on my face, dancing around the apartment to the *Pulp Fiction* soundtrack, putting on my blackest eyeliner and struggling with outfit schizophrenia. By the time Mark arrived, there was a pile of discarded clothes on the bed and I'd moved on to the more date-friendly Counting Crows.

Mark had made reservations at an adorable Italian restaurant he'd picked out in a little artist community nearby. I was thrilled about all the effort he was making. This boy was into me.

When we were seated, he ordered a bottle of wine and then looked over the menu, chatting animatedly about the things for which only single people have the luxury of passion—concerts, movies, mutual friend gossip. Not particularly focused on the food, I asked him what was good. Mark simply waved his hand in the air and said, "Order whatever you want."

Soon, my pea-sized bladder insisted I break the dreaded seal. Afterwards, I reapplied my lip-gloss and checked out my ass in the full-length mirror.

When I returned, I was surprised to find a shot glass filled with purple liquid waiting beside my already full wine glass.

Mark stood and pushed in my chair like a gentleman, picked up his shot and said, "Here's to a great night!"

*Well, that's one choice,* I thought.

But in the spirit of his toast, I tossed it back, figuring—*it's purple, how strong can it be?*

After some time had passed and I'd made a little ladylike headway into my seafood linguine, another restroom pilgrimage was in order.

The click-click of my heels on the hardwood floors signaled my return to the table. I was just tipsy enough to start feeling pretty confident in myself. I stared Mark directly in the eyes as I approached the table. He really was cute.

But before I was even completely into my chair, he lifted another shot glass into the air and enthusiastically said, "Cheers!"

"Oh!" I said, cocking one eyebrow quizzically, "Um, okaaaaay."

He just smiled and held his glass aloft for my clink.

I returned the gesture warily and put the glass to my lips, intending to take only a sip, then thought, *Eh, what the hell?* After all, I was sure my tolerance could withstand a couple of sissy shots and a glass of wine or two.

And this is when things start to get blurry.

There was another trip to the ladies' during which the bathroom bandit ordered yet a third shot. I won't even pretend to have tried to resist it in my woozy state.

There may have been more wine. I think there was an after-dinner drink somewhere else.

What I do remember clearly is that we ended up back at my apartment passionately making out, both of us pretty drunk. We were sitting on my sofa in the dark, fully clothed, when Mark took his hands off my back for a few seconds and seemed to scratch his leg furiously.

I heard jangling sounds for about two seconds and then I was enveloped in his arms and lips again.

For better positioning, I shifted my weight and then extended my right hand toward the opposite side of his waist. As I did, my arm brushed something soft and warm in his lap. Alarms went off in my head and then my elbow came to rest on what could not be denied was a pulsating piece of man flesh.

It was then that I realized Mark had not scratched his leg. Instead, he'd quickly undone his belt and zipper and released his man meat into the wild.

Yes, ladies, my gentlemanly date laid his chub in his lap for me to find, like a delightful Easter egg nestled in a bit of monkey grass.

Had all the blood drained out of his big head into his little one? What the hell was he thinking?

*Ahh, the organic twigs and berries aren't selling on the back shelf—better position them front and center where their qualities can be properly appreciated.*

Or perhaps he'd learned valuable lessons from all the porn he'd watched. Surely the mere sight of his love muscle would have me overcome by lust, unable to choose between immediately riding his baloney pony with abandon or stopping to call my girlfriend to come share it with me.

Or could it be he was afraid the metal in his zipper was blocking the signals his antenna was aiming at my mouth?

I envisioned myself leaning down and tapping the head, saying, *Hellooo? Is this thing on? What the hell do you think you're doing?* But instead, I pulled away.

Who knows where the date could've gone had it been allowed to progress in the way a normal date does?

But it didn't.

He took it out.

And I took off.

I excused myself to go to the bathroom, mouthing "Oh. My. God," into the mirror a few times and when I re-entered the room, I looked directly into his eyes and said, "It's time for me to go to bed."

He smiled. "Can I come?"

"Uh. No. At least not here."

And then, because he hadn't bothered to do it while I was in the bathroom, you know, just in case I was hungry—he stood and put his junk food back into his pants and zipped himself up while I averted my eyes.

To call him Mark is to be disingenuous because the truth is that I have no recollection of his name. For a few hours, he was "Mark," or whatever his name actually was, and then he became "He Took It Out" until the end of time.

In the park where I sometimes take my children to play, there's a pavilion where random people are always sitting, looking like they're up to something shady with cigarettes and crinkled, bottle-shaped brown paper bags.

Today, two lovebirds straddle a bench, knee-to-knee. There is little more between them than a barely concealed bottle of wine and a bit of tingly, hormonally charged air.

She leans in to him and then jumps up screaming.

And my elbow feels that phantom prick that reminds me how happy I am to be married.

*Suzanne Fleet is a writer and SAHM of two stinky boys who works hard to exercise her family's sense of humor by writing about them on her blog,* Toulouse & Tonic. *Suzanne's writing has won her numerous runner-up trophies and honorable mentions over the years. Always a bridesmaid, never a bride. Except for that time she was a bride. Connect with her on Twitter @toulouseNtonic.*

# Backflash

*by Keesha Beckford*

Wedging my little face between the bathroom door and its frame, I was able to catch a glimpse of something—something that would be burned in my memory forever. It was both glorious and frightening—the kind of thing about which anthems were written and to which men bowed down, renounced all earthly possessions and swore their eternal allegiance.

It was Auntie Cece's* big butt.

Kneeling over the tub to run her bath, Auntie Cece unwittingly offered a full view of her beyond-ample hindquarters. Most definitely, it was the biggest behind I had ever seen, especially without clothes. It was round and smooth and firm and a deep chocolate brown. Screaming, "Here I am!" it seemed to want to burst through things—the anatomical equivalent of the Kool-Aid Man.

"It's so *big*!" I whispered to my mother, who had crept up behind me to see what had me so mesmerized.

Mom snickered, grateful, I'm sure, for some comic relief, however inappropriate. Auntie Cece was my mother's oldest sister. Their father's wake had been hours earlier and the funeral was the following morning. Auntie Cece was staying with us in Queens, to avoid going all the way to Washington Heights and then coming back at the crack of dawn.

It was unkind, certainly, to gawk at a grieving person lost in a private moment. And it didn't help that my mom and Auntie Cece had been at odds throughout their lives. While my mother was petite and sensitive, Cece was voluptuous and flamboyant, the family diva. I can't help thinking that our gaping was somewhat of a delicious thrill for my mother, like attending the 20th high school reunion to find that the bitchy homecoming queen had matured into a toothless carnie.

"That's enough," my mother said after several minutes. She pulled me away from the door and sent me off to bed.

For a good while after, I felt troubled. *How on earth did anyone's behind get so huge? Would that happen to me? Would my butt be so big when I grew up?*

While my booty would never amount to Auntie Cece's ginormous gluteal orbs, it definitely would not be the ass of my dreams. Best described as a bubble, an onion or an apple, it was high and muscular, and seemed to have ambitions of being a hat. As anyone who has ever done a proper plié knows, this type of butt is the ballet student's nemesis. From the side a dancer strives to be one skinny straight line. No matter how thin or well aligned I was, it always looked like someone's basketball had bounced up and gotten stuck under my leotard. In front of whole classes, dance teachers regularly told me to tuck under, or that they could put their teacup, if not an entire set of *Encyclopaedia Britannica* on my rear end. It was beyond humiliating.

My butt was also troublesome in real life. Skirts that draped nicely in the front rode high in the back. I tried on many a pair of jeans that fit my tush, yet gaped comically at the waist. Starting in the 8th grade I began to dread going up to the board to diagram sentences or write out math problems. Thankfully the long shirts of the '80s often helped obscure my rising-skyward bubble.

Fifteen years after The Auntie Cece Incident, despite, or perhaps even because of my apple bottom, I landed my first big dance gig. I was touring Germany in the dancer chorus of a German rock opera. I had arrived! I was in Europe, dancing in stadiums seating thousands of people, and making great money for a 21-year-old. The show itself was called *Tabaluga und Lilli*, and was about a little dragon named Tabaluga, a popular German children's character. Coming up with an American counterpart is tough, but anyone who needs one should picture a folksy, kid-friendly Bon Jovi doing a rock musical about Thomas the Tank Engine or Curious George.

In one scene, Tabaluga has an unfortunate entanglement with the Black Widow Spider. In what some would find merely bizarre and others would find mind-bogglingly racist, the three other African-American women in the show and I were the Black Widow's sexy nurses. And by sexy nurses I mean hooker clowns. With bras stuffed to a size that would alarm even an ardent boob fetishist, we were costumed in tight labia-length white nurse's dresses, white fishnet stockings, and high-heeled granny shoes. We also rocked goggles and antennae.

To add to the trauma, all four of us were in the number immediately before and had a quick change to get into this nurse get-up. If quick changes were rated on a scale of measured to rushed, this one came in at bank teller-at-gunpoint. Many times we literally sprinted to our opening places, which had the four of us entering through the audience to a hexagonal platform separated from the main stage by a runway.

Our dance was treacherous and cerebral, requiring us to negotiate a web the size of the platform, a fake violin, its bow, and stairs. Fucking stairs! Even weeks into the tour, when we had done the number many times, it still unnerved the bejeezus out of me.

In this piece Auntie Cece would have her revenge.

It was a show in which we were off—very, *very* off. On our platform we could clearly see each other, something we used for moral support. This particular night, we pulled each other under like a fur coat on a drowning man. When we all stood with one leg extended high in the air, faux-stroking our violins, Nikita lost her balance and very noticeably had to put her leg down. Strike one. *Oh God . . . keep it together, keep it together*, I repeated internally. Then I watched in horror as Reneé dropped her violin down her set of stairs and had to WALK DOWN TO GET IT, like someone who'd spilled the contents of her coin purse. Strike two. Shit was getting real...must focus! Not a minute later, Michelle STUMBLED DOWN THE STEPS! Strike three. *Shit ball change!*

There was a bad case of fuckupitis going around.

Even though I was a hyperventilating nervous wreck, I soldiered on. Finally, we lay with our legs draped over our set of stairs, faux-played our violins, and threw our legs back over our heads. The end was near, and I began my internal happy dance.

*What the?!* My legs would not move. I couldn't bring them back down. I was stuck! My fishnets were stuck in my antennae. MY FISHNETS WERE STUCK IN MY ANTENNAE!

Panicked, I wriggled and squirmed. How was I going to get up? Would the number end with me showing my hoo-ha to a stadium of Europeans? Would I be carried away still in a position that looked like I was being diapered or having my temperature taken rectally? The seconds felt like hours. Just when hopelessness set in, and I was sure I'd live out my days being rolled around with a stick, I gave a delicate heave-ho and boom! My legs were free! I slipped back into the choreography and finished the number normally, to applause that felt somewhere between tepid and "you're lucky we don't have rotten vegetables."

Afterward, the four of us slunk back to the dressing room looking like we had just been horsewhipped.

"What the hell happened?" asked the other dancers, who had watched the whole debacle on the monitor.

After the shock and horror of what we'd just perpetrated had worn off, we laughed until the tears fell. Anticipating the performance notes and questions we'd get from the director the next day made us even more hysterical.

In the end, I too would know how it felt to be gawked at—to have my (albeit clothed) rump on display for, not two family members, but an audience of thousands. Interestingly enough, to this day, I don't know if Auntie Cece really had no idea my mother and I were watching her, or if she knew all along and chose to ignore us.

Either way, she wouldn't have cared. Nor would she have been overwhelmed by shame to be on stage with her fanny shining up to God and everyone. Auntie Cece wasn't the easily embarrassed type. She didn't walk around apologizing. For better or worse, she didn't much care what folks thought about her. If you didn't like her ass that was *your* problem, not hers.

And in that way, I wish I were more like Auntie Cece. At 40, for me ass pride is still a work in progress. But I'm getting closer. Closer to embracing my bubble booty. Closer to being proud of it. And most of all, closer to being supremely confident that when I exit a room, I do so in a blaze of glory.

*This story is truer than true, but names have been changed to protect the identity of one bootylicious relative, may she rest in peace, and a group of dancers who had their asses handed to them.

*Before her two children re-choreographed her life, Keesha was a professional dancer who performed in the U.S. and in Europe. Today she teaches modern and jazz dance in the Chicago area. She is also the human cyclone behind the popular blog* Mom's New Stage. *A multitasker at heart, she shows fierce skills at simultaneously writing, choreographing, checking Facebook and Pinterest updates, playing the role of a mother named Joan "Kumbaya" Crawford, and overcooking food. Her writing has been featured on* Mamapedia, The Huffington Post, *and in the bestselling anthology* I Just Want to Pee Alone. *Connect with her on Twitter @MomsNewStage.*

# Dropping the Mask

*by Angie Kinghorn*

Women have a bad habit. We think it's our job, no, our *sacred duty*, to be "fine" when anyone asks. It's especially acute in the South, where we're taught to apply "fine" like a mask when our mamas teach us the proper way to blend foundation. We're expected to wear both every day thereafter.

Even when we're crumbling to dust, crushed by grief; even when we're reduced to piles of ash by flames of embarrassment; even when we're paralyzed by the sheer weight of expectations from every corner, and the resulting guilt when we fail to meet them all—we're fine. No matter how public the pain, whether we've singed off a lock of hair with a curling iron on YouTube, or been on the receiving end of an email from the deranged sorority sister from hell or her older PTA equivalent—we're fine.

Because, dear God, what would happen if people didn't think we had it all together?

After my twins were born, I was battling postpartum depression and anxiety. Nothing in my world was fine. Every part of my body was leaking something, I didn't remember what sleep felt like, the babies crying in my head may have been real or imaginary, and I couldn't stuff myself into anything other than maternity clothes. My look was disheveled at best, and getting life under control felt like the game we played as kids, trying to grab a greased watermelon in a pool. And the thought of that made me want to cry because pools? Bathing suits? They don't let whales in either one.

And yet, I did my duty and eked out a "fine," when friends asked how I was doing. It would have been truthful, had someone altered the dictionary thus:

**Fine /fīn/**

*Adjective: Held together by Spanx and stitches that may or may not have dissolved; constantly panicking about whether said Spanx are rolling down one's waist into a conspicuous roll; taking copious amounts of Valium; using roughly double the usual amount of under-eye concealer; crying like a baby (often with a baby); being unable to remember whether teeth have been brushed, deodorant applied, or tampon changed; experiencing regular panic attacks, milk stains on shirts, and breasts so engorged they frequently swell to chin level; suffering unpredictable flashes of anxiety which lead to heavy sweating in public.*

That's right, according to that definition, I was fine.
Until I wasn't.
One day, I was so not fine that both my therapist and my husband sounded the alarm and I got into serious treatment for postpartum depression. Nobody knew, and I wanted it to stay that

way. It seemed shameful not to be lounging on pink-tinged clouds of happiness eating organic bonbons made by the unicorn I should be keeping in my kitchen—I'd just had two beautiful, perfect babies! But the shame was the depression talking, and after I got over it, I made a decision that has permanently altered my life.

I dropped the mask.

I stopped pretending things were OK when they weren't. If a close friend asked me how I was doing, I told her the raw, ugly truth.

I began to write it all on my blog, honestly, pulling no punches. Words poured out of me onto the page, bursting through the dam. It was the world's biggest therapy session, the life equivalent of punching pillows. All my anger, grief, regret, shame, and happiness (yes, I do have that, too) filled the pages and left me—not empty, but cleansed.

Bizarre things started to happen.

Women whom I'd considered very close friends, BFFs even, were uncomfortable with this not-fineness. I had broken the code. I'd suggested that this motherhood thing wasn't perfect, that, in fact, this life thing wasn't perfect. They edged further and further away, especially as I started to write about it. Many of those women are no longer my close friends, and some are now gone from my life completely.

For each of the women who've left my life, others have moved closer and opened up about their lives, complete with trials and tribulations. We talk about what we're actually feeling, and that? Feels damn good. I dropped the mask and found my tribe. Some of them live here in the real world; many of them live in my computer. But I get to see them at conferences a few times per year, and that's enough. My beautiful group of friends who want to talk about the real, open, raw, and honest parts of life and don't freak out when I'm myself. Unedited.

While I might slightly edit myself for a party with my husband's co-workers, I can't stand the stifling feeling of putting on that mask every day, and I'm certainly not wearing it to places that are my daily stomping grounds. There's no way, for instance, I'll wear it to pick my kids up from school.

One beautiful fall day on the playground after school, the conversation turned maudlin, as two of my PTA friends wondered what they would do if their husbands were to die.

"Well, thank God we've got plenty of life insurance," said one.

"No kidding," said the other. "I could go back to work, but that would be the last thing I'd want to do."

It went on in that vein for some time; the two women talking about the financial stresses they'd no doubt face, until I couldn't take it anymore.

"What about sex?" I blurted. "Wouldn't you miss sex?"

They took a step back in unison.

"Well, no," one said, "I don't think I'd miss it all that much."

"I'd just get a vibrator," said the other.

"You mean you don't already have one? How do you not already have one? I mean, they're called *marital aids* for a reason." It came out of my mouth before I could stop it, because a filter is not part of Unedited Me.

Both said remarkably Chevy Chase-like versions of, "Oh, we've gotta run, we're late for the thing at the place!" and scrammed.

This is the downside to being unedited: if you're not careful you can find yourself standing alone when your big mouth runs away and takes your friends with it.

Online is easier. There I have girlfriends with whom I can discuss everything (including sex), and it's fabulous. The other day a group of us were chatting, putting it all out there. And I do mean *all*. Tips for giving great head, recommendations for better vibrators—because we're the kind of girls who go to conferences where they hand out free vibes as swag.

The day after that fabulous online chat, I was on the playground again, talking to a different group of women, and I mentioned the online chat and how fabulous it was.

"What was it about?" asked a tall blonde.

"Everything you can imagine related to sex. Things like techniques for how to give better head, for example."

She reeled backwards as if she'd been hit. "Oh, my God!"

"What? Are you ok?" I asked.

"Yes . . . I . . . I just don't do that," she said.

"You don't give blowjobs?" I asked, incredulous.

"No, I just don't talk about it." She was bright red, and like the PTA chicks last fall, immediately remembered someplace she had to be.

Clearly I've got to work on my judgment, at least if I don't want to be a pariah by the time my kids hit middle school. The other playground moms might own vibrators and read *Fifty Shades*, but they're certainly never going to 'fess up to burning out their Pocket Rocket and ask for replacement suggestions. And if you suggest better smut for their reading enjoyment, they'll back up slowly like you're holding explosives. You've got to know your company, and I often fail spectacularly in discerning who might be receptive to what.

Unedited women are worth their weight in margaritas. They're the ones who are brave enough to show their real faces to an unreceptive world, the ones with whom you can fly your freak flag high because they've already got a flagpole in their front yard.

They'll be your life friends, the ones who know your heart, not just your living room fabrics and your china pattern.

So, drop the mask, but be prepared for mixed results. Some people will love it and you'll find your tribe. Others will listen to the real you and run like hell.

Drop the mask anyway.

It's worth it.

*Angie Kinghorn is a lifelong North Carolinian and a sorority girl turned Junior League dropout. Her work has been published in* Precipice: The Literary Anthology of Write on Edge, *and the* BlogHer 2012 Voices of the Year *compilation. She's a firm believer in God, dark chocolate, and the Oxford comma. Friends predict that the availability of Sharpies combined with society's affinity for bad grammar will eventually get her arrested. She writes at AngieKinghorn.com, and you can follow her on Twitter @AngieKinghorn.*

# Pillow Talk

*by Lori Wescott*

To be quite honest, I'm not sure when foreplay became a thing of the past rather than a vital part of the present. My husband Brantley and I are approaching the ten-year mark, so I think it's safe to say that *something* is working. The seven-year anniversary came and went without so much as an itch, which means we must have had some sort of precursor to the down and dirty back then. However, my brain is not the steel trap it used to be. I constantly have to remind myself what day it is, so trying to remember the last time someone else took off my clothes is a lost cause.

I will be the first to tell you that I've never been big on romance. The one and only time Brantley bought me a sweet, sentimental Valentine's Day card my response was, "Gross. Get a room." That was the last time we pretended to celebrate what I now refer to as "VD." I could spend an eternity talking about that ridiculous, made up holiday, but I won't. Not today.

Try as I might to remember from whence it departed, the fact remains the same. Foreplay in our marriage has been substituted with a variety of phrases that Brantley uses when he really wants to woo me into the bedroom.

The most recent occurrence went down like this. Our son had just gone to bed and Brantley and I were watching TV on the couch. He gingerly reached over and placed his hand on my thigh as he whispered in my ear, "Mind if I run one up in you?" It may be hard to believe that I didn't actually melt into a puddle of lust on the floor. He took my blank stare as a "yes" and ran to the bedroom shouting, "I bet I can be naked before you can!" He won that contest.

"I almost broke my neck tripping over your clothes," I said in an unsexy voice. "I know," he said. "It was a booby trap! Now, get over here and let me see them titties." That night we made love in my favorite position: the Johnny Come Quickly. It was magical.

Not to sell my husband short, he has several other "come hither" lines that send tingles up my spine—not really good tingles, but the kind of tingles you get when you see a middle-aged man lurking around a playground or a four-year-old being breastfed in public. I've been wooed with phrases such as, "Mind if I stick it in you," and "What do you say we head up to the bedroom and I lay the pipe to you?" What girl could say no to that? My all time favorite lines are the ones he manages to word in such a way that I wind up feeling special. Those instances vary, but generally sound something like, "If you're really good and don't gripe too much about me staying at the gym for four hours, then I just might come home and lay the wood to you."

You may disagree, but I assure you that I'm not here to bash my husband. I know full well that foreplay is a two way street and that I could certainly put forth more effort to make it happen. However, this is where my principles get in the way. I pride myself at being a champion of mediocrity. If there's any half-assing to be done, you can rest assured that I will find it and blow it *almost* out of the water.

So in all fairness, here is a list of my faults:

1.) As I already stated, I do not have a single romantic bone in my body. I have never been, and never will be, the girl who wants someone to gaze adoringly into her eyes.

2.) I'm fairly reluctant when it comes to grooming my bearded dragon. I can definitely see why Brantley may want to limit the amount of time he has to look at the beast dead-on. This leads me to my next point.

3.) I have a busted vagina. No matter how you dice it, I was ripped asunder in childbirth and the only thing that could make it more ugly would be an actual zipper.

4.) Another result of child bearing is the severe 'Rhoid Rage I was left with. You've never seen *The Grapes of Wrath* until you've taken a look at my undercarriage.

5.) I'm not great at dirty talk. It just isn't something I can do without laughing. The closest I've ever come to successful dirty talk was, "I haven't taken a real bath in three days." Neither of us was happy I said it.

6.) Then, there is plain old exhaustion. It's hard to clean the house, cook meals, clean again, play with the offspring, and have a warm and bubbly personality by the time the husband gets home from work.

7.) Brantley's long work hours and the frequency with which he has to travel also severely limit our together time. Oh wait, these are supposed to be my faults. Well, you can't hide from the truth.

Regardless of who's at fault, if Brantley and I don't change something in the bedroom soon, then this temporary rut could become a permanent ravine. I don't want us to be the couple who drop off their kid (and the only thing they still have in common) at some college orientation a few years from now. "Pardon me, have we met? You remind me of someone I hooked up with about eighteen years ago."

We have a fun homework assignment ahead of us and I'm certainly up for the challenge. A girl can only hear, "What do you say I lay the pipe to you?" so many times before she loses what few faculties she has left and beats her husband to death with an actual pipe.

Operation Foreplay, commence.

*Note: In order to acquire my husband's blessing for the telling of this story, I had to agree to mention his "enormous cock." Please stretch your arms as wide as they can go. It's *that* big.

*Lori Wescott is a thirty-something humorist and freelance writer residing in Music City. She is the creator of Awkward Smoking Pictures, which you can find among other places, on her blog Loripalooza—Where Funny Rocks. Her work has appeared in* Chicken Soup for the Soul: Family Matters, *as well as various newspapers. She's been named Trophy Wife of the Year for ten years in a row according to one website (hers). When she's not writing humor you can find her writing indie music reviews, falling down in public and taking care of her ginger son, Luke. Follow her on Twitter @LoriWescott and visit her blog* Loripalooza.com.

# A Vagina Full of Love

*by Julie C. Gardner*

The framed cross-stitch on the wall above my head says this: *The world is full of beauty when your heart is full of love!*

I, myself, am fully reclined, feet in stirrups, thinking: *That's delightful! But what about when your vagina's full of speculum?*

Of course I don't say these words out loud. Instead, I answer the string of questions posed by my gynecologist, a gentle woman with a soft voice and even softer hands.

(Don't be jealous.)

*Yes, my cycles are still regular. Sure, I do monthly self-exams on my breasts. No, I don't drink more than two glasses of wine in one sitting. Maybe I always tell the truth. Sometimes.*

The doctor asks me to scoot (even) closer and, for the 26th time since I slipped a half-gown over my whole-body, I reassure myself that my lower portion can't be the worst thing she's seen today.

After all, I'd showered up and trimmed before my appointment. I was nothing if not well-groomed in anticipation of a virtual stranger coming at me with a Q-tip and gloved fingers.

But then I found myself in the waiting room (wearing my best panties beneath a sundress that's easily removed) flipping through someone else's discarded tabloid. And those slick, hyped-up pages treated me to rumors of one celebrity's Botox. Another actress's lip implants.

A Real Housewife's vaginal rejuvenation surgery.

*Wait. She put the who in the what now?*

My thoughts, exactly.

Which is why, despite the real risk of permanently tainting my Internet browser (no pun intended), I Googled that shit the minute I got home.

Vaginal. Rejuvenation. Surgery.

(Side note: Most sites display pictures and now I can't uncross my legs.)

Now, before I comment further on another woman's choices, I'll admit I've taken liberties with my own secret garden.

Quick story:

When I was 19-ish, I bought a *sexyatthetime* bathing suit from Body Glove that grew too sheer when wet. It was 1988, so the Brazilian wax was not yet a twinkle in some salon technician's eye. Hell, even porn stars sported merkins. (Google it. With pictures!) Faced with a paucity of options, I sought the advice of my charming *boyfriendatthetime* who suggested I dye my situation a subtle platinum to render it practically invisible, plus also *hawt*. (He then suggested that he watch.) But despite careful supervision, I was left with what looked like a patch of neon-yellow highlighters between my thighs. Then, in a stroke of regrettable timing, I found myself in a group shower with his mother that same week. (We were camping and yes, it was as awkward as it sounds, playing *Julie and the Amazing Technicolor Dream Crotch* alongside women who hadn't trimmed their own bikini lines since the Nixon administration.)

But I digress.

Because my basic point is this: I do not judge.

If you want to play around with your vulvar region for practical purposes or fun—for entertainment or pleasure—go for it, you little vixen. Get your kicks.

But before you pay someone to approach you with real, live surgical equipment, be mindful of your true motivations.

Pap smear = good for you.

Jailbait labia = very, very bad.

Seriously, ladies. Haven't we subjected ourselves to enough unrealistic expectations about aging? The wrinkles above my knees are plenty discouraging. Don't tell me I'm now supposed to question the excess baggage in my personal claims department.

Please.

I've long labored under the delusion that anyone who's been issued a passport below the equator should be happy to be invited in the first place. Are we to now assume that a daily shower and a once-over with a Daisy Razor will no longer satisfy future visitors?

Perish the thought.

It's not like I'm a prude who's anti-experimentation. Oh, no.

I like to bring the spice as much as the next Real Housewife.

As evidence, I present the time I tried to give my husband a Millennial Thrill for Y2K by shaving off the whole enchilada. (So to speak.) *Won't he be surprised?* I thought. And he was, just not quite pleasantly. After a quick peek, he said I resembled our six-month-old daughter whose diaper he'd just changed.

And that, ladies and gentleman, is how to kill a New Year's Eve.

But I digress (again).

Because my point is that this failed attempt to push the envelope (so to speak) was merely superficial, cheap and temporary. A topic for our turn-of-the-century conversation.

Fast-forward 13 years and women are going to increasingly extreme measures to prune their land down under. We no longer simply vajazzle the joint. We're being told to permanently youthen it. (I know *youthen* isn't a word, but it should be. After all, it's a movement poised to undermine the confidence of every single female who's currently aging. Which is, for the record, all of us.)

Instead of treating our bodies like amazing vessels of life, we look for new ways to laser, pluck, pierce—even slice—the parts that thrive there.

Why, oh why, do we do this to ourselves?

To each other?

To (no, NO, *NO!*) our daughters?

I have grown two human beings in this space. I pushed their tiny (and yet somehow enormous) forms through an impossibly small venue, then nursed each one of them for a full year. In the years since, I've strived to make both their lives and mine stimulating. Enriched. The stuff of fairy tales and college acceptances.

But now, in a doctor's office I entered to pursue health, I'm tempted by a magazine to add this to my list of concerns:

*Have my genitals reached their expiration date?*

It's madness, I tell you. Clitoral madness.

And it must stop.

I'm not suggesting we give up all manner of grooming in one fell swoop. I don't own a see-through bathing suit these days, but I do still swim in public. I'll continue to keep Sasquatch at bay with a Lady Bic before donning this season's Target two-piece.

But beyond that, I'm requesting a permanent cease-fire on all our various nooks and crannies. Let's celebrate the ins and outs of ourselves, treat kindly those glorious folds that say:

*I am WOMAN and you're damn lucky to love me. Even if I'm saggy.* Because I am so much more than my body. My sexuality. My shallow surfaces.

You are, too.

And then there's this:

I want my daughter to cherish every part of her; to celebrate her strengths and not be critical or—even worse—*desperate* to prove her worth, in the face of perceived flaws.

Yes, I have a vagina and a brain, of course. A heart. These are concrete.

I also have hopes and dreams, a restless soul that's ever-changing. Why shouldn't my physical self be allowed to mature alongside an abstract spirit?

It's time we embrace authenticity with open arms. But please, nobody point out the "bingo wings" while we're at it.

I do not want my kids to navigate this world believing they or the partners they choose are less than or too much...or perhaps *enough* but still *not quite exactly right.*

No, I hope our children can love themselves and others based on criteria that truly matter.

I want them to enjoy youth but also respect age and wisdom. Maybe even grace.

And if they're going to learn, the lessons begin here. With you. With me. I'm ready to start teaching now.

Armed with a heart full of hope and a vagina full of love.

(So to speak.)

*Julie C. Gardner is a former English teacher and author currently working on her second novel. The mother of two perpetually embarrassed teenagers and wife to one long-suffering husband, Julie was a* BlogHer *Voice of the Year in 2012. She also enjoys cheese more than most people. You can find @JulieCGardner on Twitter or visit her blog,* By Any Other Name, *at* JulieCGardner.com.

## About the Editor

*Leslie Marinelli is a writer, editor, wife, mother of three, toilet humor aficionada, and transplanted Pittsburgher trapped in the suburbs of Atlanta. She's a weekly columnist and the Editor-in-Chief of* In The Powder Room, *as well as the creative force behind the riotous blog* The Bearded Iris: A Recalcitrant Wife and Mother Tells All. *Leslie was named a* BlogHer *Humor Voice of the Year in 2013 and 2012, and a* Babble *Top 100 Mom Blogger in 2011.*

*For more of the best and bravest female writing online join us at*

**www.InThePowderRoom.com**

*From there you can also connect with us on Facebook, Pinterest, and Twitter @InThePowderRoom.*

59808234R00145

Made in the USA
Columbia, SC
08 June 2019